OPTIMAL IMPERFECTION?

OPTIMAL IMPERFECTION?

Domestic Uncertainty and Institutions
in International Relations

GEORGE W. DOWNS
DAVID M. ROCKE

PRINCETON UNIVERSITY PRESS
PRINCETON, NEW JERSEY

Published by Princeton University Press, 41 William Street,
Princeton, New Jersey 08540
In the United Kingdom: Princeton University Press, Chichester,
West Sussex

Library of Congress Cataloging-in-Publication Data

Downs, George W.
Optimal imperfection? : domestic uncertainty and institutions in international
relations / George W. Downs and David M. Rocke.
p.   cm.
Includes bibliographical references and index.
ISBN 0-691-04460-0
ISBN 0-691-01625-9 (pbk.)
International relations—Political aspects. 2. International relations—Economic
aspects. 3. Political stability.   I. Rocke, David M., 1946– . II. Title.
JX1395.D69   1995
327.1'01—dc20   95-11312

This book has been composed in Computer Modern using the TEX/LATEX
typesetting System

The publisher would like to acknowledge the authors of this volume for
providing the camera-ready copy from which this book was printed

Princeton University Press books are printed on acid-free paper and meet the
guidelines for permanence and durability of the Committee on Production
Guidelines for Book Longevity of the Council on Library Resources

Second printing, and first paperback printing, 1997

Printed in the United States of America
by Princeton Academic Press

10 9 8 7 6 5 4 3 2

FOR ILENE AND CARRIE

Contents

List of Figures

List of Tables

Preface

One of great insights of classical realism was that uncertainty about power and about the evolution of power is as important in shaping the ecology of international relations as the distribution of power itself. In this book we attempt to demonstrate that an equally significant part of the impact of domestic politics on international relations springs from the institutional responses that domestic uncertainty inspires.

These responses are often missed because institutions are treated as exogenous or simply part of the strategic environment rather than as strategies themselves. This is particularly true of those domestic institutions associated with democracy that are believed to influence the character of the international system. Scholars are quite willing to believe that a law requiring legislative concurrence for a declaration of war reduces the incidence of interstate conflict, but they rarely entertain the possibility that such laws exist primarily to reduce domestic uncertainties like those associated with executive motivation.

International institutions are more likely to be recognized as strategies than are their domestic counterparts. Until relatively recently, however, the impact attributed to domestic uncertainty in shaping the character of these institutions has been minuscule compared with that of system structure or even uncertainty about state power. Yet the more closely one examines institutions such as GATT, NATO, or the Montreal Protocol, the more it becomes apparent that key aspects of their structure function to cope with one or more of the many varieties of domestic uncertainty. Whether one can make the teleological leap to argue that these institutional details have been consciously designed to deal with the problems of uncertainty depends on the particular details of each case. It is not difficult to believe, however, that in the absence of uncertainties about domestic politics, such institutions would operate quite differently.

In our exploration of the effects of domestic uncertainty we rely on a variety of incomplete information games. Although the use of such games has become standard practice in international relations, those employed here tend to differ in a number of ways from the standard extensive form signaling game with which many readers are familiar. First, we employ models that often allow continuous, rather than binary, responses. This more realistically represents the choices available to the actors in many arms, trade, and environmental situations. Second, we allow many kinds of uncertainty in our various models; not only uncertainty about what the other parties have done and about the payoff functions of the other parties, but also about the present and future capacity of other states to carry out the terms of the agreement. This greater flexibility in modeling results in conclusions that should be more robust than those from more limited efforts.

We would like to extend our appreciation to those friends, students and colleagues who have been interested enough and kind enough to wade through the various drafts of this manuscript or otherwise to offer helpful suggestions. These include Steve Brams, Bruce Bueno de Mesquita, Kimberly Elliott, Josh Epstein, Joanne Gowa, Mel Hinich, Keisuke Iida, Arie Kacowicz, David Lalman, Jean-Pierre Langlois, Ariel Levite, Michael Lewis-Beck, John Londregan, Jim Morrow, and several anonymous referees. Ken Oye has been invaluable not only in providing detailed comments, but also in keeping us aware of the larger messages that can easily be lost in the tangle of modeling concerns. Peter Barsoom provided detailed comments and helpful references from the political economy literature. Malcolm DeBevoise offered helpful editorial advice and coordinated numerous matters with his colleagues at Princeton University Press. We are grateful to the University of Texas Press for permission to use material from the *American Journal of Political Science* (Downs and Rocke 1994) in Chapter 3. Finally, Ilene Cohen ably demonstrated that good copyediting is not a lost art.

OPTIMAL IMPERFECTION?

Chapter 1
The Impact of Uncertainty

Incerta pro nullis habentur.
(The uncertain is counted as nothing.)
   —Legal Maxim

1.1   Introduction

During the past decade scholars have become increasingly convinced
that "domestic politics matters" in international relations. Unfortunately, there has not been a corresponding increase in understanding
just *how* domestic politics matters. This book joins a number of recent
efforts to remedy this problem by focusing on the impact of a particular
facet of domestic politics, in this case domestic uncertainty.[1] It deals not
so much with the errors in judgment that domestic uncertainty causes
as with the institutional consequences of knowing that such errors are
possible and their effects on the international system. To use an analogy
from the world of medicine, it focuses less on the fact that uncertainty
causes misdiagnoses than on the fact that the existence of such misdiagnoses is likely to bring about the establishment of institutions such
as malpractice insurance and second opinions, which in turn have their
own implications for the cost and quality of medical care.

   Malpractice insurance and second opinions, though not institutions
in the sense of being formal organizations, are a kind of institution that
will play an important role in the chapters that follow. They are *endogenous* in the sense that they represent strategies that actors consciously

---

[1]See, for example, Bueno de Mesquita and Lalman (1992); Iida (1993); Mo (1994);
Milner and Rosendorff (1994); Morrow (1991); Fearon (1994); and Hess and Orphanides (1994)

adopt to deal with the recurring, potentially problematic situations created by uncertainty. Once adopted, such strategies then play a significant role in structuring the incentives that influence behavior. When these strategies remain stable over time—or, more precisely, when they meet the technical requirements of being equilibrium strategies in repeated games—it is appropriate to consider them institutions in the sense that they constitute society's "rules of the game" or "humanly designed constraints that shape human interaction" (North 1990, 3).[2]

The impact of uncertainty is often underestimated because of the tendency to treat institutions as exogenous and part of the strategic environment. When this is done, any effect that uncertainty might have on policy vis-à-vis its impact on institutions disappears from the analysis. To continue with the medical analogy, uncertainty will appear to play a smaller role in a system of medical care that has board certification, malpractice insurance, and second opinions than in one that does not. Worse, the more the influence of uncertainty is embodied in institutions, the more its effects will tend to be concealed by the assumption that institutions represent nothing more than interests or constraints.

The range and diversity of institutions that influence the international system and whose design is, in turn, influenced by domestic uncertainty is vast. They include formal treaties and organizations like the GATT or NATO, and the thousands of less formally codified norms that help govern interstate behavior. They also encompass those institutions *within* states that play a major role in shaping international relations.

While an important part of our analysis lies in the explication of how these institutions benefit states by mitigating uncertainty's ill effects, none is completely successful. Uncertainty plunges us into the world of the second best and no institutional mechanism, no matter how cleverly designed, can replicate the efficiency gains that would be achievable in an environment of perfect information. It is this inevitable imperfection that led us to choose the title for the book. Second opinions, for example, lower the cost and increase the effectiveness when the correct diagnosis is uncertain, but they increase the cost over what it would be if the nature of the disease and the character of the best treatment were known. While it is helpful to know that a perfect solution to the problems posed by uncertainty is unachievable, it is also desirable to know just how

---

[2]For more extensive discussions of the game-theoretic perspective on how institutions should be defined, see Schotter (1981) and Calvert (1992).

imperfect a particular institutional solution happens to be. This will lead us to focus on the imperfections and spillover costs of the institutions we examine, as well as on the benefits they provide.

Interestingly, while according to our definition, institutions may appear to include virtually anything of interest to a political scientist, past studies of uncertainty have virtually ignored them. Until the twentieth century, most observations about the role of uncertainty in international relations dealt with its implications for strategy in transitory situations, especially the initiation and conduct of war. The ancient Chinese warrior-philosopher Sun Tzu, for example, explored how leaders could exploit uncertainty during battle and how they could increase it when it was to their advantage. Hence, many of his maxims dwell on the role of spies, deception, and surprise attacks (Sun Tzu 1991). Thucydides, for his part, was less interested in the tactical utility of manipulating uncertainty than in its power to undermine the best-laid war plans. Presaging the coming conflict, he repeats Athenian warnings to the Spartans that a protracted war would invite the unpredictable and put both their fates at the mercy of accident (Thucydides 1972, 98).

Machiavelli, writing almost two millennia later, appears to have been among the first to venture beyond the connection between uncertainty and war to speculate about its implications for the conduct of state policy more generally. However, his prescriptions were often profoundly noninstitutional. For example, believing that some portion of human destiny could be controlled, Machiavelli challenged the common belief that fate was all, and he adjured leaders not to turn their destinies and those of their states over to chance. A better strategy, he argued, is never to commit oneself to a single ruling style: "For if time and circumstance are favorable to one who acts with caution and prudence he will be successful, but if time and circumstances change he will be ruined, because he does not change his mode of procedure" (Machiavelli 1950, 93). Unfortunately, Machiavelli offered little advice about how the prince should decide when to change his style or about the consequences that such a fickle regime might have on the actions of other princes.

It was not until hundreds of years later, in the middle of this century, that attention began to shift to the role of different types of uncertainty in determining the operation of the international relations system. The early realists who emerged in the wake of the Second World War were intrigued by the implications of capability uncertainty for geopolitical strategy. More recently, the psychological school of international relations has looked at implications of various cognitive heuristics and biases employed by decision makers to cope with uncertainty. The focus and methodology of this book, however, are quite different.

Unlike either classical realist theory or the psychological school, we will focus on the many uncertainties that arise from domestic politics. Voters are uncertain about the degree to which their elected officials share their policy preferences and about how to prevent these officials from using privileged information for their own private purposes. Elected officials, in turn, are uncertain about how current commitments will restrict their ability to respond to the contingencies posed by shifting domestic coalitions of interest groups and economic conditions. Diplomats are uncertain about the impact of changing domestic politics in other states on the willingness and ability of these states to meet their commitments. We will show how these uncertainties and others like them structure the incentives and constraints that determine the general configuration of international relations.

We will rely on noncooperative game theory to help us understand the expectations that domestic uncertainty creates and the consequences of that uncertainty. A special strength of this methodology is that it allows us to consider the reciprocal effects of uncertainty on strategy in a systematic fashion. It enables us to take account of the fact that actors are able to intelligently evaluate each other's motivation and strategy and use the results to guide the design of their institutions. The logic embodied in this method often rests on complicated mathematics, but the payoff it yields is often superior to that obtained by more intuitive methods. Early realists, for example, tended to believe that uncertainty afforded states numerous opportunities to inflate their reputations. The reasoning was simple, straightforward, and, as far as it went, impeccable: in the absence of high-quality information about military strength, a state can pretend to have soldiers and weaponry it does not actually possess, or it can overstate the capability of those it does possess. By implication, the power of a substantial number of states is likely to be inflated at any given time and weak states have a great deal to gain by pretending to be strong.

Game theory tells us that this reasoning can be misleading because it neglects the fact that states are likely to develop strategies to cope with the uncertainties they know to be present. The calculating state understands that uncertainty provides the opportunity for attempts at misrepresentation. It therefore knows that it should discount self-generated claims of strength on the part of states in the same way a bank officer discounts a loan applicant's self-assessment of his or her solvency or the implications of the expensive (borrowed? counterfeit?) watch on the client's wrist. True, the weak state can also act like a strong state, but the wise state knows this, too, and can discount actions as easily as talk. In fact, the application of these sorts of calculations reveals something realists tended to ignore: uncertainty may cause the most problems by making it difficult for a strong nation to convince other states that it really is strong unless it takes very costly action (Nalebuff 1991).

The book unfolds in the following way. After reviewing research on the impact of uncertainty in this chapter, we describe in Chapter 2 the logic of noncooperative game theory under incomplete information. Because the topic is so broad and because so many fine texts have recently been published, our treatment is necessarily summary; it highlights a few archetypical models that have important applications in international relations. Our treatment differs modestly from those in the basic texts in that our examples emphasize the operation of Bayesian learning more than do conventional examples, where play quickly "degenerates" into a separating or pooling equilibrium. As a result, our approach requires the use of more complicated extensive-form games than is usual, but we believe that it is important to appreciate both the consequences of policy makers having to use inference to resolve uncertainty and what is needed to control the pace of its resolution. Only historians and political scientists with the confidence born of hindsight possess the gift of recognizing an "implacably revisionist" state the moment it appears.

In Chapter 3, we examine a dimension of uncertainty that originates in domestic institutions and affects the international system through them. This is the voters' uncertainty about the extent to which their executives conduct foreign policy in the manner they desire. How can voters insure that their executives do not exploit their information advantages to formulate policies that are more passive or more aggressive than they would desire? The topic is not only of substantive importance for a society that is still arguing over the degree of misrepresentation involved in Vietnam and the Iran-Contra Affair, but it also represents a sharp departure from the unitary actor model that critics wrongly believe is intrinsic to formal modeling.

In Chapter 4, we consider the impact of various kinds of uncertainty on the institutions that states establish to maintain international agreements. Most interesting is how decision makers' uncertainty about the demands of special interests within their own and other states leads to the establishment of institutions that appear inefficient but actually are not. Thus, as we show, the penalties embodied in institutions such as GATT and Super 301 represent "fines" for defection that are high enough to prevent the abuse that would exist under a casually policed system of diffuse reciprocity but also low enough to allow liberal states the benefits of bowing to the demands of key constituencies without risking a trade war. We then demonstrate that this strategy does not depend on a mutual vulnerability to protectionist forces. Even if a powerful state is fully committed to free trade, the presence of protectionist interests in a weaker state may lead to the establishment of an institution that stops far short of enforcing free trade. This is because the free trade state, knowing that the weaker state will still violate the free trade norm, calculates that the cost of having to impose the penalty is not worth the benefit.

In Chapter 5, we explore the institutional consequences of uncertainty about a state's present and future capacity to implement the domestic regulatory provisions of a multilateral agreement. That such uncertainty is endemic in the international system is incontrovertible. Apart from the issue of state preferences, no one is certain whether Thailand and Indonesia will be able to control the devastation of their rain forests; whether China will be able to enforce the intellectual property provisions of the new GATT; or whether Eastern European states will be able to control their air pollution problems. These kinds of uncertainty have enormous consequences for the design and operation of international institutions, and they play a prominent role in the calculations of every good policy maker. Oddly, however, their impact is rarely if ever explicitly modeled.

The context involves two states trying to decide whether to invite a third, less economically developed and more politically unstable state to join them in the creation of a trilateral institution designed to reduce pollution in a body of water that borders all of them. The two states are convinced that they both have the capacity to implement the domestic regulatory rules that the institution might make but they have doubts about the third state's capacity to do so, and they believe that whatever its present capacity might be, it is likely to change in the future, quite possibly for the worse. Our analysis reveals that while the first type of capacity uncertainty can make the third state's admission into the institution problematic, the second type will often make it impossible. This turns out to have significant implications for the distribution of different size institutions in the international system and for the strategy that a group of activists might use when attempting to establish an effective regulatory regime.

1.2 Realism and Early Rational Choice

Predictably, early realists were preoccupied primarily with the uncertainty involved in the estimation of power, the basic building block of realist theory. The more closely they examined the historical record, the clearer it became that states were often uncertain about both their own power and that of other states. As in the case of the First World War, the experience of the Second World War suggested that none of the obvious indicators was a particularly reliable predictor of the power that the states were able to marshal (Aron 1973, 57–58). Contrary to expectations, gross national product did not work well because its components exhibited a highly variable capacity to be mobilized for a war effort and because a state's ability to translate economic potential into military strength was affected by elusive factors—the ability of a given population to redistribute itself across new job categories and to engage in self-sacrifice, for example. Still further complicating the translation process were idiosyncratic aspects of timing and geography that could never be anticipated before the outbreak of a conflict.

Realists theorized that the uncertainty connected with measuring power has various effects. For one, it encourages the use of surrogate measures of power that may themselves be imperfect or biased. Political consensus, for example, is a tempting indicator of a state's willingness to fight, but it is biased in favor of autocratic regimes because they do not have to cope with a free and critical press (Aron 1973, 61). Uncertainty also makes it possible for a state to overstate its own as well as its rival's power. Although this overestimation frequently induces dangerous miscalculation, it can sometimes provide a state with the advantages of boldness. A state that believes itself more powerful than it actually is acts more adventurous—and, up to a point at least, may mislead other states about its relative power (Organski 1968, 109).

Morgenthau speculated that because no state can be certain of its relative power each must seek a margin of safety. As a result states are less interested in "balancing" than in achieving a measure of superiority. "Since no nation can foresee how large its miscalculation will turn out to be, all nations must ultimately seek the maximum of power obtainable under the circumstances. Only thus can they hope to attain the maximum margin of safety commensurate with the maximum of errors they might commit" (Morgenthau 1973, 208). The uncertainties associated with the reliability of one's allies in the event of war further increase the incentive to achieve a comfortable superiority.

The deterrence problems created by uncertainty about relative power were only compounded by the additional uncertainties connected with nuclear weapons. The superpowers had created a world that appeared to rely on the threat of a punishment that would be suicidal to carry out. This paradox of deterrence, as it came to be called, perplexed realists until the economist and game theorist Thomas Schelling proposed a rationale for its success that did not focus on the plausibility of threats and credibility. The key, he argued, lay in the existential deterrence created by the knowledge that when states increased their military preparedness for war during a crisis, they also increased the possibility that there would be accidents that might lead to inadvertent war. "The choice is unlikely to be one between everything and nothing. The question is really: is the United States (in response to a crisis) likely to do something that is fraught with the danger of war, something that could lead—through a compounding of actions and reactions, of calculations and miscalculations, of alarms and false alarms, of commitments and challenges—to a major war?" (Schelling 1966, 97).

Schelling was also concerned about the incentives that uncertainty provided for risk taking. A threat to start a nuclear war might be unconvincing because of its suicidal nature, but a state that can convince its adversary of its willingness to incur a small increase in the possibility of an "inadvertent" disaster has a powerful coercive tool by which to compel other states to act according to its wishes. More than at any time in the past, willingness to engage in risky behavior and resoluteness in the face of risk promised in the nuclear age to compensate for a relative absence of capability.

For Schelling and others, the game of chicken captured the dynamics of the new nuclear world. States embark on trials of brinkmanship or are thrust by fate into unavoidable contests of strength that neither can avoid. The object is to reveal which state has the most nerve: the state that hangs in the longest—as the United States did in the Cuban missile crisis—wins the spoils. Just as important as any immediate prize, however, is the reputation gained, with its future value as bargaining leverage in the hundreds of conflicts of interest that will inevitably arise.

Uncertainty makes it difficult for a state to withdraw unilaterally from a game, even though some view it as needlessly dangerous. In a world of uncertain intentions and commitments, both boldness and timidity signal rival states about how aggressive they dare be in making demands. When a state attempts—for whatever reason—to "drop out," the adversary tends to infer that there is profit to be made by making bolder demands. "It might be hard to persuade the Soviets, if the United States yielded on Cuba and then on Puerto Rico, that it would go to war over Key West" (Schelling 1966, 124). This is why states fight over obscure parts of the world. "Few parts of the world are worth the risk of serious war by themselves, especially when taken slice by slice, but defending them or running risks to protect them may preserve one's commitments to action in other parts of the world and at later times" (ibid.).

The critical role that uncertainty plays for realists is evidenced in their internecine quarrels as well as in their theory. When, despite their shared emphasis on capability and its determinants, realists have disagreed about doctrine, it has often been the case that the disagreement hinged on the role of uncertainty. Bueno de Mesquita (1985) has observed that much of the debate between the faction of realists who contend that multipolar systems are more unstable than bipolar ones and the faction that takes the opposite position is actually a debate about the effects of uncertainty. While both sides begin by assuming that multipolarity induces uncertainty and bipolarity induces certainty, the minority faction, represented by Deutsch and Singer (1964), assumes that uncertainty inspires cautious behavior. Most of the field, like Waltz (1979), argues that uncertainty produces dangerous miscalculations that can undermine the balance of power.

In retrospect, it seems clear that some of the difference between the two sides is the result of confusing actual probability with subjective probability. It is true that people act cautiously when they feel uncertain, but it is also true that they make the most serious miscalculations when the estimate of uncertainty they use in their decision calculations is incorrect. Deutsch and Singer are making a statement about how uncertain people behave; Waltz is telling us about the consequences of making mistakes and the inevitability of such mistakes occurring in an uncertain world.

The debate can be framed differently: if we assume that states are risk averse, they will increasingly "discount" the expected value equivalent of uncertain payoffs. In this narrow sense they can be said to act cautiously in the presence of uncertainty. But uncertainty also affords states attractive opportunities to pretend to be more powerful than they are, and it can lead them to think that misbehavior has taken place when it has not. How do these countervailing forces balance out, we may wonder? Will risk-averse states succumb regularly to the temptation to inflate their reputations? Will the consequences of imperfect information be trivial or major?

These kinds of questions can be adequately addressed only with the aid of a methodology like game theory and a particular model that explicitly incorporates the recognition that states formulate strategies by considering prospective actions of other states. A state's ability to exploit an uncertain environment to inflate its reputation is obviously bounded by a rival state's awareness of the same uncertainty and the way that it can be manipulated. Similarly, the potentially negative effects of imperfect information are mitigated by the awareness on both sides that it is imperfect. We need a technique that can quantitatively characterize these boundaries and how they shift as information is gathered. With such a tool we can move from Machiavelli's abstract prescription that the prince remain flexible to the critical determination of when the prince can reasonably conclude that circumstances have changed enough to warrant modifying his ruling style. We will also be able to refine the intuition of modern realists like Organski who believed that a state's overestimation of its own power could lead either to dangerous miscalculation or disproportionate influence, but who had little to say about when one or the other was likely to occur.

Theorists such as Powell (1990, 1992, 1993) have already begun to reformulate realist theory so that it is consistent with the precepts of noncooperative game theory, and eventually it may help us understand how domestic uncertainty and capability uncertainty are related. After all, theorists such as Aron and Morgenthau understood better than anyone else that some states were more capable than others of translating their industrial strength and manpower into military might. This was why they stressed that measurement of power is uncertain and worried about its implications. The realists were just not certain how, if at all, this uncertainty was affected by domestic politics. There is, however, more to the impact of domestic politics and domestic uncertainty than its effect on how states estimate power.

Whatever the loss in explanatory power caused by the omission of domestic-level variables when we are trying to account for the number of great power wars or the relative stability of bipolar and multipolar systems,[3] it is clearly dramatic when we are trying to account for the evolution and character of the world's trade regime or the effectiveness of efforts to limit ozone depletion. Economic development and relative capability—the classic indexes of power—cannot begin to explain the

---

[3]The most systematic analysis of the limitations of realist theory in regard to great power war and system stability is contained in Bueno de Mesquita and Lalman (1992).

variation in the institutions that states employ or the outcomes that are achieved. Unlike many critics of realism we believe this inability is evidence not so much of the theory's fundamental weakness as of the fact that it was designed to explain other things. Nonetheless, the fact remains that we need to look elsewhere for inspiration in trying to understand how domestic politics influences international relations.

1.3 The Psychological Tradition

We have seen that for realist theorists, the effect of uncertainty is the residue of the rational, self-interested actions that state decision makers take in trying to cope with it. Reason dictates that responsible decision makers react to the ambiguity of power by creating a margin of error; it also inspires states to seek qualitative rather than quantitative focal points when trying to tacitly coordinate their actions in an uncertain environment.

Researchers influenced by cognitive and social psychology take a different approach, viewing responses to uncertainty as shaped less by rational calculation than by psychological biases and heuristics that lead states to misperceive the actions and motives of their rivals. For example, one such source of misperception, termed the *fundamental attribution bias* leads individuals to view their own actions as highly constrained responses to factors outside their control but to view the actions of others as the result of unconstrained choices (Heider 1958; Ross and Anderson 1982). Holsti, along with many others, argues that such were the dynamics leading up to the First World War. Each state believed that it and its allies were highly constrained and had no choice but to take extensive defensive measures, while the other side was free to make the modest conciliatory gestures that could have prevented war. The refusal of the other side to make such gestures served to confirm suspicions of aggressiveness (Holsti 1972, 167–68). The result, the psychological tradition contends, was a needless war that flies in the face of the prediction of deterrence theory that high expected costs and balanced forces should prevent conflict.

Throughout the 1970s and 1980s, a host of researchers investigated the implications for international relations of a wealth of specific heuristics and biases uncovered by experimentalists, as well as the implications of more general psychological theories (e.g., attribution theory, schema theory, prospect theory). The psychological processes themselves are the focus of this research—some of these studies do not even mention the word uncertainty—but uncertainty about the intentions of a rival creates the inferential puzzles that the heuristics resolve. The effect of increased uncertainty is thus the sum of the psychological tendencies that it unleashes.

Collectively, these tendencies act to reduce instrumental rationality, inhibit signaling, and limit the decision maker's understanding of how and why other states make decisions. In the process, they reduce the predictive power of rational or realist models of deterrence and crisis decision making, and consequently they reduce the ability of strategies derived from them to maintain peace. Early adherents of the psychological school rejected the strategy of deterrence in its entirety and sought to introduce what they referred to as "assurance strategies." These approaches to reducing tension might consist of a single gesture designed to cut the Gordian knot of fear and distrust (e.g., Sadat's trip to Israel) or a more complicated strategy, such as Osgood's GRIT (graduated reduction in tension), that prescribes modest and increasingly generous unilateral gestures of cooperation designed to initiate a spiral of cooperation.

An institutionalized reliance on assurance strategies makes sense if we can be certain that both sides in an international conflict are motivated exclusively by security interests. In such a world, miscalculation and unjustified insecurity are the only things to worry about, since calculated aggression or attempts to obtain the policy leverage so often associated with military advantage are simply illusions. Unfortunately, as most contemporary researchers in the psychological tradition now acknowledge, aggressiveness is not born solely of insecurity. Britain's failure to engage in military preparation convinced Argentina's military junta that there was no reason not to launch the attack that precipitated the Falklands War (Stein 1991), and the same thinking process arguably lay behind the Iraqi invasion and occupation of Kuwait, the event that precipitated the Gulf War. We are left with a situation in which there is little reliable guidance about "whether to try to seek to prevent miscalculated escalation through restraint or to deter a premeditated challenge through threat and demonstration of resolve" (Stein 1991, 37).

Obtaining such guidance depends on having (1) an understanding of how and to what extent counterproductive heuristics and biases can be overcome and (2) a methodology that helps us understand the implications of complex strategic interactions. That dysfunctional heuristics and biases can be partly eliminated is a matter of record. Individuals can be trained to take account of base rates rather than ignoring them, just as they can be trained to overcome some of the problems of "unwarranted" loss aversion by thinking in terms of final rather than interim gains and losses. Institutions exist to encourage such learning. Insurance companies use computers, actuarial tables, and financial incentives to overcome the base rate problem. Financial institutions have used similar techniques to deal with endowment effects and loss aversion. While it may not be as straightforward a matter for policy-making institutions to overcome the negative effects of the fundamental attribution problem or loss aversion, surely some learning can take place. Indeed, it is the possibility of learning that presumably justifies the use of GRIT in the first place and motivates members of the psychological school to share their research findings with government officials.

What are the implications of such learning for foreign policy strategy? Why would a state aware of the potential perversities of psychological heuristics assume that its rival is not? How does one estimate the degree to which a rival state is driven by strategic considerations rather than by psychological processes? Do some types of states learn more quickly than others? Can one state help another state learn to overcome various heuristics and biases?

The psychological school has no real answers to these sorts of questions. Just as early realist scholars could provide relatively little guidance to decision makers about how they should go about making inferences with regard to reputation or credibility, international relations scholars in the psychological tradition have yet to come up with a methodology capable of guiding decision makers in making inferences about a rival state's motivation or the extent to which an assurance strategy can be exploited.

This is true of even the most ambitious attempt by the psychological school to move from the enumeration of individual heuristics to a more integrated theory. This involves applications of *prospect theory*, so called because it deals with the evaluation of alternatives or prospects under uncertainty. Originally set forth in a 1979 article by Daniel Kahneman and Amos Tversky, prospect theory was developed as an alternative to standard expected utility theory as a descriptive model of decision making under risk. One of its components is the *certainty effect*, which postulates that people place a lower value on outcomes that are probable and a higher value on outcomes that are certain than standard utility theory would prescribe. A second component is the propensity of individuals to evaluate outcomes from a reference point or anchor that is often, but not always, the status quo.

The contention that there is risk aversion in choices involving sure gain and risk seeking in situations where there are sure losses is supported by a wealth of experimental evidence. If people are given the choice between a prize of $3000 and an 80 percent chance of winning $4000 dollars, they overwhelmingly choose the first alternative, despite the fact that the expected value of the second choice is $3200 dollars. In itself this is no particular surprise; it has long been suspected that people tend to be risk averse. What is interesting is that if the same individuals are given the choice between losing $3000 dollars for certain or an 80 percent chance of losing $4000 dollars, they will even more overwhelmingly choose the latter, risk-seeking choice (Kahneman and Tversky 1979, 268). This suggests that their utility function is not purely concave in the way we associate with risk averseness but rather concave with respect to gains and convex with respect to losses.

According to prospect theory, individuals evaluate gains and losses from a reference point that represents either the status quo or an asset position that they expect to attain. Given the shape of the utility function, departures from the reference point in either direction are considered to be inferior to their comparable expected value. This implies the existence of an *endowment effect* by which people value something they possess more than they value an equivalent good that is not in their possession. Another is the phenomenon of loss aversion—that the loss of a prize of a given size carries more pain than its acquisition brings pleasure.

As Levy makes clear in an excellent review essay (Levy 1992a), there is an abundance of experimental and anecdotal evidence in support of both the endowment effect and loss aversion. Experiments such as those where students were found to demand compensation to give up a good (e.g., a coffee mug) that was often several times larger than what they were willing to pay to purchase an equivalent good corroborate the endowment effect, as does the general tendency to overvalue out-of-pocket expenses in comparison with forgone opportunities for gain. The principle is even embedded in legal doctrine, in the distinction between "loss by way of expenditure and failure to make a gain" (Levy 1992a, 175). Loss aversion is suggested by evidence ranging from people's preference for low and zero deductibles (Kahneman and Tversky 1979, 269) to statements such as that by Jimmy Connors, "I hate to lose more than I love to win" (Levy 1992a, 175).

Prospect theory appears to be consistent with a broad spectrum of international relations behavior. Jervis argues that loss aversion, in particular, helps explain a wealth of phenomena. The asymmetry of the domino effect, for example, by which decision makers appear to fear that the effects of small losses will be greater than the effects of equivalent size gains is a simple extension of loss aversion, as is the related tendency to consider the significance of their own losses to be far greater than the significance of losses of a similar magnitude experienced by their rival (Jervis 1992, 189).

Loss aversion and risk averseness in seeking gains combine to suggest that interstate violence is inspired more by the expectation of loss than by the anticipation of gain. It predicts the prevalence of preventive wars and leads us to expect, correctly as it turns out, that defensive motivations of the type that led Japan to attack the United States are more common than the expansionist dreams that motivated Hitler (Jervis 1992, 194). It also suggests that the strategy of deterrence gets an extra boost from the fact that both states are often operating from a reference point that is defined by the status quo. Potential aggressors will therefore be less likely to initiate conflict than a pure expected-value calculation would suggest because risk averseness acts to discount the expected gain and loss aversion inflates the value of the expected losses.

The downside, according to prospect theory, is that if deterrence breaks down, the chances are not good that the ensuing war will remain limited (Jervis 1992, 194). Loss aversion will motivate the state that finds itself losing to adopt ever riskier escalatory strategies rather than end the conflict with a modest loss, and the winning side will quickly adjust its reference point to reflect recent gains, thus limiting its receptivity to compromise proposals. If neither side gains an advantage, the situation will be no better. The losses suffered by each side in what has so far been a draw will propel both of them to eschew a truce and adopt even riskier strategies. Thus loss aversion provides an explanation for the "inexplicable" carnage and duration of "hopeless" battles and campaigns in World War I, World War II, and the Iran-Iraq War, as well as in a host of civil wars.

Loss aversion has implications for bargaining as well as conflict. As Levy notes, "If actors in a bargaining situation treat their own concessions as losses and the concessions they receive from their adversary as gains, they will overvalue the concessions they make to the adversary relative to the concessions they receive from their adversary" (Levy 1992b). This, in turn, reduces the size of the bargaining space and the likelihood that a peaceful resolution will be achieved. In those cases where the two sides are bargaining over the distribution of losses, the situation is especially bad.

Prospect theory is a provocative alternative to conventional utility theory, but it has yet to be developed to the point where it can serve as a theory of foreign policy decision making. One critical problem flows from the fact that there is no theory of "framing" that tells us how and where the reference point is established. The status quo is an obvious choice, but there are many situations in which the influence of expectations is critical. A state that expects a debtor state to default on its loan may well view a partial payment as a gain. A state that expects a state to repay the loan in full will view such an outcome as a loss. Which one is correct? What is the source of these expectations? Can one state strategically shape the expectations (e.g., the reference point) of another to gain advantage? If so, how?

Those in the psychological school argue that rational choice theorists cannot answer such questions either. Even if this were true, however, it would be a frail defense of prospect theory. Fortunately, it is also largely incorrect. The reference point for rational choice is established by rational expectations that are, in turn, determined by the outcome of utility-maximizing strategic behavior within a game. Given some knowledge of initial beliefs, the game theorist has a well-defined procedure for determining how both the lending state and the debtor state should act and can generate a forecast about what will happen. In short, rational choice does have a theory of how (and when) the reference point and frame shift.

Prospect theory—at least to date—can do none of these things because like conventional utility theory it is a theory of choice, not a theory of strategic behavior. Even if psychologists manage to replace conventional utility theory with prospect theory, they will still need to employ a methodology that can help decision makers cope with the complex strategic inferences generated by uncertainty. Today there is only one such methodology—noncooperative game theory.

In order to help us understand the impact of domestic uncertainty, the psychological tradition will also have to start taking domestic politics more seriously. Developed in large part as a critique of classic realism, the psychological tradition has to some extent allowed its aspirations to be defined by its opposition. Thus, the vast majority of books and articles using this perspective focus on the ways that heuristics and biases alter the perceptions and behaviors of individual decision makers coping with issues related to conflict and deterrence. These works are as detached from trade and environmental issues as is realism, and they have just as little to say about why institutions are structured in the way that they are and what impact they have.[4]

1.4 The Institutionalist Tradition

During the 1980s international relations scholars shed much of their cold war preoccupation with traditional security topics and moved on to such areas as international trade, development, human rights, regional integration, and the environment. One of the consequences of this new interest was that it brought them into contact with a wealth of formal and informal institutions that played little or no role in the realist or psychological paradigms. To help understand their function and operation, the scholars looked to what is termed the *institutionalist perspective* or the *new economics of organization*—a loose composite of transaction cost economics and the noncooperative game theory described in the next chapter.

The two schools of transaction cost economics that influenced international relations researchers both emphasize the importance of uncertainty in motivating the creation of institutions and determining how they are structured. The first, associated with the work of Williamson (1975, 1990), Coase (1937), and Commons (1934), is primarily concerned with replacing the abstract black box representation of the firm found in microeconomics with a fuller theory that tries to account for variations in firm structure. Its foci are the myriad transactions that constitute the internal and external activity of an organization (e.g., gathering information, negotiating agreements, collecting payments due) and the ways in which the cost of these transactions affects firm and industry structure. Uncertainty figures prominently in the theory because it is among the most important determinants of these transaction costs. The volatility and uncertainty of markets increases the costs of marketing and gathering information, for example, and uncertainty about the training and reliability of personnel increases supervisory costs.

Because it increases transaction costs, uncertainty shapes firm structure. The classic example is the choice between a structure dependent on a decentralized system of exchange based on legal contracts, on the one hand, and one that depends on formally integrating different activities within the confines of the firm, on the other. As various sources of uncer-

---

[4]Several notable exceptions can be found in Stein and Pauly (1993).

tainty converge to increase the complexity of possible contingencies, the costs of devising contracts to cover these uncertain transactions become increasingly prohibitive and contracts become ever more "incomplete" in relation to what is needed to define fully the structure of the relationship. Organizations find that they can operate more efficiently by incorporating such transactions within their own boundaries through vertical integration or—more relevant to understanding the genesis of cooperation in the international system—by devising some system that permits ongoing collusion (Helfat and Teece 1987). This imperative created by different varieties of uncertainty is the dominant determinant of organizational structure: "The differences among simple market contracting, complex contracting, vertical integration, and other ways of organizing transactions lie primarily in the institutions they specify for governing the relationship when circumstances not foreseen in the contract arise" (Milgrom and Roberts 1993, 62).

For this school of transaction cost economics, the presence of "asset-specific investments" serves to magnify the effects of uncertainty by increasing the vulnerability of the actors. These investments are specific to a particular contract or context, such as a set of employee skills or a particular machine that is critical to the conduct of business in a given firm, and they are rarely required elsewhere. The limited demand means that the supplier of the good or service in question must either be unusually confident that she will have a long-term relationship with the firm or be able to devise a contract that compensates her for ongoing training and development costs. One valuable option that may accomplish both and lower transaction costs in the process is to incorporate the development of the good or the training of the person within the boundaries of the firm. The more uncertainty there is about the future of either the firm that supplies or uses the asset-specific investment, the more this is likely to be done.

Asset specificity has proved to be useful in understanding phenomena like the evolution and structure of international trade regimes. For example, Yarbrough and Yarbrough (1992) argue that asset specificity is one of the two principal determinants of how trade regimes are structured. If a state can simply shift its trade from one state to another state on roughly the same terms, trade can proceed with little attention to the possibility of a breakdown. Uncertainty is low and a state can unilaterally lower tariffs without fear of exploitation. Under these circumstances, no trade regime is necessary.

If trade is based on some asset-specific investment (e.g., an expensive plant or pipeline), the same flexibility is absent. Canadian automobile parts plants designed to serve the needs of U.S. automakers cannot easily shift to the task of supplying parts for German companies. In order for these sorts of investments to be made, there must be minimal uncertainty about tariffs (and property rights). This requires effective third-party enforcement by a hegemon interested in free trade (e.g., the United States after World War II), some sort of safeguard (provided by linkages or "hostages"), or an effective multilateral trade regime.[5]

The second school of transaction cost economics is exemplified by North (1981, 1984, 1990), Barzel (1982, 1989), Cheung (1974, 1983), and Milgrom and Roberts (1990, 1993). It devotes particular attention to "bargaining costs." These are defined broadly as "the opportunity costs of bargainers' time, the costs of monitoring and enforcing an agreement, and any costly delays or failures to reach an agreement when efficiency requires that all parties cooperate" (Milgrom and Roberts 1993, 72). Bargaining costs are the appropriate locus of attention, the argument goes, because they are what necessitate the creation of incomplete contracts. A la Coase, adherents of this school argue that if bargaining costs were zero, one could always design an efficient contract.

Whether this shift in emphasis from incomplete contracting to bargaining costs is as fundamental as the second school suggests is arguable, but as a practical matter its members have tended to focus greater attention on enforcement problems and on the evolution of mechanisms to deal with them. Thus, North and Weingast (1989) discuss the situation before the Glorious Revolution: opportunistic appropriation by the monarch, together with ambiguous land titles and contract law, acted as a drag on institutional performance. The result was an uncertainty discount that inflated the cost of property and goods for wary buyers. This held down the rate of economic activity and the rate of economic growth. The Glorious Revolution led to various political reforms, including laws establishing the supremacy of common law courts. This effectively insulated the courts from the monarch and the nobility and fostered more secure property rights. The rapid growth of a capital market and the development of banking followed and together became the engine that powered the creation of a colonial empire.

[5] For another application of asset specificity to trade policy, see Frieden (1991). For an interesting study of what happens when institutional rules fail to perform their function of maintaining openness, see Oye (1992).

Whereas the institutionalized coercion represented by the English court system is a relatively straightforward method of reducing the costs of uncertainty, other methods operate more subtly. Consider the body of commercial law established by merchants during the early Middle Ages. Though designed to cope with many of the same constraints confronted by international institutions, on the surface at least, its basic character-istics would seem to doom it to impotence. It was privately operated; it received no financial assistance from any state; and its judges had very limited powers of enforcement. Yet despite these limitations, the court was a success, not because it devised some alternative enforcement mechanism, but because it disseminated information about reputation. Merchants found it in their self-interest to use the judges' rulings to structure their future business dealings because that reduced the level of uncertainty about other merchants' honesty and dependability more re-liably than could have been achieved through the unstructured diffusion of information. High-quality information about reputation combined with self-interest led merchants to behave more honestly, to participate in sanctioning violators, and even to pay judgments against them that were personally costly (Milgrom, North, and Weingast 1990).

This interest in enforcement issues drew the North school toward modern industrial organization theory and noncooperative game theory upon which it is based—a rather ironic development. Both schools of transaction cost economics had, after all, seen themselves initially as a part of a behavioral economics movement that emphasized the inade-quacy of classic industrial organization. The explanation for this turn of events was largely methodological. During the 1970s and 1980s spe-cialists in industrial organization found in the theory of repeated games and incomplete information intuitively appealing answers to a number of problems that had previously been the province of transaction cost economists. At the same time, behavioral economics was foundering in its search for ways to formalize concepts like satisficing, problemistic search, and aspiration level. Such events prompted transaction cost economists to become interested in noncooperative game theory. As they came to acknowledge its instrumental value, they began working with industrial organization specialists.

The same synthesis took place in the international relations commu-nity. Theorists such as Keohane (1984) were quick to appreciate the relevance of the new institutionalist economics and game theory for the study of regimes and cooperation, and to recognize the connection be-tween international institutions and the problems posed by uncertainty.

They emphasized that in areas like trade, finance, transportation, and communication, states had much to gain if uncertainty about how other parties would behave could be resolved (1) through the systematic collection and dissemination of compliance information by an international institution comparable to the medieval court and (2) through the establishment and dissemination of procedural and compliance norms. Quite obviously, institutions that provided these services offered substantial efficiency advantages over a system that required ad hoc bargaining each time a good was traded, currency was transferred, two ships found themselves on a collision course, or a telegram was sent.

Nevertheless, few of the early works inspired by the new institutionalism dealt with domestic uncertainty and its effects. Scholars simply assumed that high transaction costs were endemic to the international realm and would continue to exist until mitigated by the emergence of some suitable international institution. They rarely mentioned the possibility that the magnitude of these costs and the difficulties associated with their amelioration might be determined by variations in the domestic characteristics of states.

1.5   Recent Research

One would have expected the institutionalist synthesis of transaction cost analysis and game theory to be enthusiastically adopted by the legion of researchers who began to rally to the banner "domestic politics matters." Yet, until recently they have generally been interested in other matters. One large faction has, like some members of the psychological school, been more interested in revealing the inadequacies of realism than in building an alternative theory. As a result, the body of research they have produced is made up largely of case studies whose only common element is evidence that some (never mind what) domestic characteristic or interest group played a major role in determining foreign policy and that the policy was inconsistent with what realism would predict. This group has little familiarity with either the theory or the methodology of the new institutionalism, and there is little attention to uncertainty.

A second faction of the domestic politics matters school has focused on the effect of democracy on a state's conflict behavior. This group is more theoretically ambitious than the first and attempts to generalize about both the character of the "democratic effect" and the mechanism through which it operates.[6] Like the first, however, it gives short shrift

---

[6]See, for example, Bueno de Mesquita and Lalman (1992) and Russett (1993).

to the role of domestic uncertainty and the effects of the institutions used to cope with it.

Attention to domestic uncertainty had to await the appearance and development of a third faction of the domestic politics matters school whose approach is explicitly game theoretic. This is the "two-level game" faction, which attempts to explain bargaining outcomes at the international level (level I) by modeling the strategic implications of the bargaining game between state leaders and their domestic constituencies (level II). In the original article describing the logic of the approach, Putnam (1988) argues that domestic uncertainty in the form of uncertainty about the range of agreements that will be approved by domestic constituencies (i.e., the size of the win set) has a variety of implications. It gives, for example, plausibility to a negotiator's claims that her ability to grant further concessions is less than what another state might have originally believed. This will act to increase that negotiator's bargaining position. On the other hand, this uncertainty also increases the other state's concern about the possibility that the negotiator's state may not live up to the terms of the agreement. This will lead the second state to demand more generous side payments, which leaves the negotiator worse off (1988, 453).

Putnam's speculations are informal and anecdotal. He makes no attempt to see whether the effects he described actually hold in equilibrium. Recently, however, many other authors have applied more formal methods to two-level game problems. Milner and Rosendorff (1994) consider the effect of legislative strength on interest group influence and find that when it is weak, the role of the interest groups will be more pronounced. Iida (1993) compares the consequences of two kinds of incomplete information that have their roots in domestic politics: "incomplete information at the international level" (or international asymmetric information), which refers to the common situation where an administration knows the preferences of its domestic interest groups but the states with which it is dealing do not, and "incomplete information at the domestic level," which describes the situation where the administration (as well as other states) are uncertain of interest group preferences. Iida finds the latter to be particularly important because it leads to the conclusion of fewer agreements as well as to a greater number of unproductive negotiations.[7]

---

[7]It might seem obvious that a decrease in the number of agreements would imply a larger number of unproductive negotiations but this is not necessarily so. The former could simply result from fewer equally productive negotiations (Iida 1993, 418).

Also in the two-level game tradition, Mo (1994) explores how uncertainty affects the use of domestic constraints as an endogenous strategy. He examines the not uncommon situation in which a negotiator has the ability to create a domestic constraint. In investigating when this strategy is profitable, Mo finds that it is often attractive because it transmits information that would otherwise be lost and because it can function to reduce the range of proposals that the other state can make.

Mo's introduction of the endogenous strategy approach brings the two-level game approach closer to the spirit of the new economics of organizations than the work of other authors who tend to view domestic politics as exogenous. For the latter, domestic politics might be constraining or unconstraining, certain or uncertain, but they are fixed. Leaders can use another state's uncertainty about what these domestic politics are to increase their bargaining leverage but they cannot alter them. Mo realizes that matters are not so simple. Leaders can, for example, release information that energizes particular interest groups, but they can also conceal information to silence others. They can create tacit bargains that require no formal legislative concurrence, or they can create formal treaties than require the assent of large legislative majorities. While one could argue that some degree of legislative assent is always necessary, this misses the point. Different paths of implementation have different transaction costs connected with them and this inevitably affects the likelihood of passage. A state leader plays a prominent role in defining which path will be chosen.

1.6 Conclusion

There is no shortage of theories about the ways that uncertainty influences the relations among states and no lack of appreciation of its importance. Classical realists argue that uncertainty about the capabilities of other states provides a sufficient condition for arms races and a necessary condition for war. Those in the psychological school believe that needless conflict and competition arise when decision makers resolve uncertainty with their judgment clouded by numerous cognitive biases.

Yet however helpful these theories might be in understanding some aspects of uncertainty, they have little to say about the role of domestic uncertainty, nor are they based on a methodology that can explicate the strategic interaction that takes place between decision makers who know enough to consider the implications of the fact that the other side is just as calculating as they. As a result, the question of how and with what consequences for the international system states employ institutional strategies to cope with domestic uncertainty has remained largely unexplored.

Chapters 3–5 contain three models that will address this question in quite different contexts. As will become quickly obvious, the approach they embody lies squarely in the tradition of the new economics of organization or neoinstitutionalism. Although no special familiarity with game theory is necessary to follow the general thrust of the arguments or the examples used to animate them, their real persuasiveness lies in the logical integrity of the different formal models they employ. The next chapter, designed for the reader who is familiar with elementary game theory but who knows little about principal-agent problems, renegotiation proofness, or trigger strategies, presents a brief overview of many of the concepts that underlie the three models.

Chapter 2
Game Theory and Uncertainty

Would you buy a used car from this man?
—Mort Sahl

2.1   Modeling Uncertainty

It is impossible to provide in this short chapter an adequate technical introduction to game-theoretic treatments of uncertainty or even an adequate review of the many applications of incomplete information models to international relations published in the last five years. It is possible, however, to provide a guide that outlines some of the major avenues of inquiry and their more prominent applications. Although a certain amount of mathematics is necessary to orient readers to the basics of modeling uncertainty, our emphasis will be on the logic that underlies the techniques. Readers who want a fuller version of the techniques described and want to learn how to apply them are urged to consult any one of a number of excellent, recently published texts.[1]

We will focus on three broad categories of models: (1) signaling games; (2) principal-agent models; and (3) models of imperfect information.[2]   The first is quite common in the international relations literature, the other two far less so. Individually, they can help us understand the interaction of incentives and uncertainty in many of the phenomena that international relations specialists find most interesting.

---

[1]See Fudenberg and Tirole (1991); Gibbons (1992); Morrow (1994); Myerson (1991); Osborne and Rubinstein (1994); and Rasmussen (1989). For more specialized treatments of incomplete information models in political science, see Banks (1991) and Calvert (1986).

[2]There is considerable overlap in the ideas that underpin these categories of models. We find it useful to distinguish between them because they are designed to deal with quite different substantive problems and they utilize different formal techniques.

Collectively, they can help illuminate the role of uncertainty in shaping the basic character of international relations.

2.2 Games of Incomplete Information
2.2.1 Introduction

Incomplete information models, of which signaling games are an important subset, are designed to explore the consequences of uncertainty about characteristics that potentially influence one state's strategy in dealing with another. The fact that this might be almost anything—the resoluteness of an ally, the ambitions of an opponent, the strength of a potential hegemon, or the commitment of an administration to peacekeeping—makes it a very flexible tool.

Following Harsyani (1967), we model uncertainty about characteristics of the other player by imposing a random move by an additional player called Nature. At the beginning of the game, Nature randomly selects the player'(s) characteristic(s) from a specified distribution. This realized value is often referred to as the player's type. In symmetric incomplete information games players begin with knowledge of their own type but know only the distribution from which their opponent's type was drawn. In asymmetric games the uncertainty lies only on one side and both players are aware of this.

A player determines her initial move on the basis of her private information and her beliefs about the other player's type. These beliefs are updated as the game unfolds by observing the other player's moves and making Bayesian inferences about the private information that motivates them, given the initial distribution from which they were drawn and given all strategic considerations.

If, in equilibrium, different types of opponents employ different strategies, their private information is completely revealed by their actions. The result is known as a *separating* or *screening equilibrium.* If different types of opponents choose identical strategies, the result is a *pooling equilibrium* and no information about the players' types is conveyed by their actions. If, as often occurs in the real world, different types of players sometimes act the same and sometimes act differently, we have an equilibrium variously known as *partially separating* or *semiseparating*, in which some but not all of the player's private information is revealed to the opponent.

These distinctions are important, because the amount of private information revealed in equilibrium is often critical in international relations. Consider reputation. In the case of a pooling equilibrium, where both a strong and a weak state choose the same strategy, the result tells us nothing about relative strength. Hence the event has no consequences for reputation. The estimates of strength that existed before the game still stand.

By contrast, games with separating equilibria provide a reliable opportunity to assess reputation. The resultant equilibrium, in which strong states always distinguish themselves from weak states, divides the two types of states into the same groups that would have existed under perfect information. This does not mean, however, that the initial uncertainty or private information was irrelevant, because the uncertainty characteristically forces the stronger state to take some costly step that a weak state cannot afford. This proves that it is strong and keeps the weaker state from reaping the same reputational benefits. This step is known as a *costly signal* and as we shall see in section 4, the ability to identify it is the key to unraveling reputation when there is an incentive to misrepresent one's type.

To appreciate the substantive significance of pooling and separating equilibria, consider Figure 2.1. It depicts a trade game where the players' actions consist of a decision of state B as to whether to impose a tariff and state A's response. Assume that A's preferences depend on its type in the fashion shown in the figure and that A's type is initially unknown to B, although B has an estimate of the probability p that A is of type 1. The choice of A's type is the move by Nature described above. Its status is unknown to B as denoted by the dotted line around Nature's choices.

First, notice that if B chooses to impose a tariff, then A will respond with its own tariff, since that produces a preferable outcome for A whatever type A is. This means that B's choice to impose a tariff produces a predictable payoff of -2. Now suppose that B contemplates not imposing a tariff. Then A's response, and consequently B's payoff, depends on A's type and on the values of a and b. Suppose that $a = 0$ and $b = 1$. Then both types of A will cooperate and not impose a tariff, so B's payoff will be 2. Similarly, if $a = 3$ and $b = 4$, then neither type of A will cooperate, so B's payoff will be -4. In either of these situations, the payoff for cooperation is predictable, and B will choose to cooperate (in the first case) or defect (in the second case) merely by comparing the sizes of the certain payoffs. Both of these are pooling equilibria, since the actions do not depend on the type, and B gains no information about A's type from observing its actions.

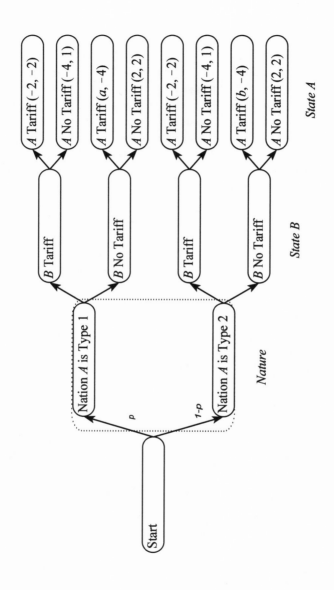

Figure 2.1: Trade Game (First Version)

Now suppose that $a = 1$ and $b = 3$. This means that an A of type 1 will cooperate in response to cooperation, whereas an A of type 2 will defect regardless. This has two consequences for B's analysis of the situation. First, B's preferred action will be determined by p, since that payoff to B for not imposing a tariff is $2p - 4(1 - p) = 6p - 4$. This is greater than -2, the payoff to B for imposing a tariff, whenever $p > 1/3$. Second, A's type is revealed completely by the action chosen, so that B is now certain of A's type.

These conveniently simple outcomes, in which either no information or all information is revealed by a choice, are a consequence of the simplicity of the game model. Aspects of the game specification that affect the pooling or separating nature of the equilibria and that could be changed to make the game more realistic include the following:

1. There may be more than two types, even a continuum of types.
2. The choices A makes may be affected by nonrepeating random (and nonobservable) events, so that predicting choices perfectly is not possible.
3. A may have more than two choices.

2.2.2 Bayesian Updating

The technology that a player relies on to update her beliefs about the type of player she is dealing with as the game unfolds is Bayes' theorem. If p is the prior probability of an event F (e.g., A is of type 1) and if another event has possible outcomes $E_1, E_2, \ldots, E_n$ (e.g., different tariffs to impose), of which E_j actually occurred, then the posterior probability (that A is of type 1 given that she chose to impose tariff E_j) under Bayes' theorem is given by

$$\Pr(F|E_j) = \frac{\Pr(F \cap E_j)}{\Pr(E_j)}.$$

Figure 2.2 shows a second version of the trade game. Suppose that the two types of A are tough, meaning that the government can stand up relatively well to domestic pressures, and easy, meaning that it is very susceptible to industry pressure. This leads us to expect that in the context of the game, an easy A will find it more painful to follow up a cooperative gesture with cooperation when there is domestic pressure. Domestic pressure may be absent, present, or strongly present, with respective prior probabilities q, r, and $1 - q - r$, respectively. As before, B's payoff for imposing a tariff is -2, because this is always followed

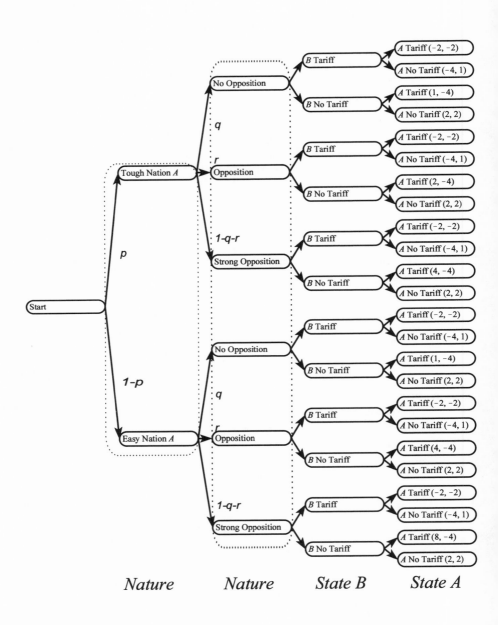

Figure 2.2: Trade Game (Second Version)

by A also imposing a tariff. If A is tough, then A will cooperate unless domestic opposition is strong, so B's expected payoff for cooperation is $2(q+r)-4(1-q-r) = 6(q+r)-4$. If A is easy, A only cooperates if there is no opposition, so B's expected payoff for cooperation is $2q-4(1-q) = 6q - 4$. Thus B should cooperate if

$$\begin{aligned} p[6(q+r) - 4] + (1 - p)[6q - 4] &> -2 \\ q + pr &> 1/3. \end{aligned}$$

Now consider what B knows of A's type after the conclusion of the game. Assume that B has cooperated. If A defects, then either A is tough (probability p) and the opposition is strong (conditional probability $1 - q - r$), or A is easy (probability $1 - p$) and there is opposition (conditional probability $1 - q$). The prior probability of A defecting is thus $p(1-q-r)+(1-p)(1-q) = 1-q-pr$. Consequently, the posterior probability of A being tough given that A has defected is

$$\Pr(\text{Tough}|\text{Defection}) = \frac{p(1 - q - r)}{1 - q - pr},$$

which is clearly always less than p. For example, if $p = .4$, $q = .2$, and $r = .7$, then the posterior probability of A being tough given defection is $(.4)(.1)/(.52) = .077$. Similarly, if A cooperates, then

$$\Pr(\text{Tough}|\text{Cooperation}) = \frac{p(q + r)}{pr + q},$$

which for the example values used is $(.4)(.9)/(.48) = .75$.

If the trade game in Figure 2.2 is played only once, there is no reason for A to dissemble, but in repeated play A may not respond "honestly." This is because A's play affects not only the payoffs in the current round but also B's opinion of A's type, which in turn affects play in subsequent rounds. If A may be playing in a way that is not myopically optimal, then B must also take this into account in updating beliefs about A.

Suppose that p is small enough that $q + pr$ is barely larger than $1/3$, so that B is just willing to risk cooperation. If A should defect, then the posterior value of p will decline and $q + pr$ will fall below $1/3$. Then, in the next round, B will be unwilling to risk cooperation, A will realize this, and both will be stuck in a cycle of costly mutual defection. All of this may be a sufficient disincentive for A not to defect in the first place.

To handle this situation formally, first calculate the value of the game to A. If B and A defect, the value is -2. If B cooperates and A is tough, then the value of the game after A observes the level of opposition is 2 (no opposition), 2 (opposition), and 4 (strong opposition). This means that the value of the game to A ex ante is $2(q+r)+4(1-q-r) = 4-2(q+r)$. Similarly, for an easy A, the value of the game is 2, 4, and 8 in the three cases, so the ex ante value is $2q+4r+8(1-q-r) = 8-6q-4r$. In either case, this is higher than -2, which is the value of mutual defection, so it is in A's interests to continue cooperation.

One strategy that A could pursue that would avoid the problem of ending up in permanent defection is always to cooperate when defection would drive p below the critical threshold. This would sometimes lead to decisions that are not myopically optimal, but the overall payoff may be higher. First, suppose A is tough. Then A needs to make a non-myopically optimal decision only when there is strong opposition. The payoff for cooperation in that case is 2 compared with 4 for defection. However, the benefit is that continued cooperation is possible. If discounted by δ per period, the benefit to the cooperative strategy in later periods is $2(\delta + \delta^2 + \ldots) = 2\delta/(1 - \delta)$ and the benefit to defection is $-2(\delta + \delta^2 + \ldots) = -2\delta/(1 - \delta)$, so the loss of 2 on the current round is worthwhile so long as $4\delta/(1 - \delta) > 2$ or $\delta > 1/3$. Since this value of δ corresponds to an interest rate of 67 percent, this condition should usually hold.

For an easy A, the cost of cooperation is 2 if there is opposition and 6 if there is strong opposition. The payoffs to continued cooperation and continued defection are the same as for a strong A, so the condition required for A to cooperate in the face of strong opposition is $4\delta/(1-\delta) > 6$ or $\delta > .6$, corresponding to an interest rate of 40 percent.

Thus, if the future is not too discounted, an equilibrium is formed by A and B behaving as in the one-period game, except when A's defection would cause p to be revised below the critical cooperation threshold. In that case A cooperates, B now gains no further information because both types behave the same, and cooperation continues indefinitely.

This introduces a common complication to equilibrium analysis. Under this equilibrium, neither a tough nor an easy A will defect in the face of the chance that B will revise p below the critical level. This is then an event of probability zero, and any attempt to use Bayes' rule to update p when A defects produces indeterminate results. The necessity to respond to situations that have a prior probability of zero has resulted in a proliferation of equilibrium concepts designed to insure rational behavior in the face of the impossible (Fudenberg and Tirole 1991; Myerson 1991).

We prefer to handle this sort of situation by redefining the game model to reflect the fact that defection is not really impossible, merely unlikely. This seems reasonable, since any particular specification is only an approximation of reality. In the trade game, this can be easily done by supposing a rare level of opposition (superstrong opposition) that provides an incentive to defect too strong to ignore. For reasonable values of δ, a payoff of 100 would be sufficient to overcome the benefit of all future cooperation. In this case, B would update p using the chances of this rare outcome, which might or might not produce an equilibrium of perpetual defection depending on the exact problem specification and on p.

2.2.3 Signaling and Reputation

The analysis of reputation in the context of incomplete information games begins with Selten's (1978) Chain-Store Paradox. The context is a situation in which a long-run incumbent firm faces potential challenges from a number of short-run firms that will each play the game once and can observe the outcome of each other's play.[3] The entrant can choose to enter or stay out of the market, the incumbent can choose to accommodate the smaller firm or to challenge it. There are two types of small firms: a tough type that will enter regardless of what the incumbent chooses to do and a weak type that will enter only when there is a good chance that the incumbent will not fight. Each entrant's type is private information but the incumbent knows the proportion of tough entrants and weak entrants. The incumbent's payoffs are common knowledge.

The payoffs and the distribution of tough and weak entrants are structured such that if the game is played only once it is rational for the incumbent to choose to accommodate. If the game is repeated with an infinite time horizon, there are a number of equilibria including one that is far more attractive to the incumbent from an expected value standpoint: the incumbent fights any challenge and no weak entrant challenges the incumbent. The attractiveness of the latter derives from the fact that whatever the incumbent sacrifices by "irrationally" fighting a tough challenger is more than made up by the benefit of scaring off weak opponents.

All of this sounds sensible enough. What is not quite as sensible is that if the game is played any finite number of times, the sole equilibrium

---

[3]This is a variant of the original game found in Fudenberg and Tirole (1991, 369ff.).

consists of repetitions of the one-shot strategy— the incumbent accommodates every round. This is counterintuitive because a many-period finite game would appear to hold the same potential benefits for the incumbent's adoption of the aggressive strategy as would the infinite game, and because people in experimental situations do not play the game in accordance with the finite equilibrium. Nonetheless, the finite solution rests on the same backward induction that usually serves game theorists so well. Since the last round (n) of any finite game is equivalent to the one-shot game, the incumbent is bound to accommodate on that round. Given that this is the case, potential entrants know that the incumbent has nothing to gain in period $n-1$ by fighting. The same holds true for $n-2$, and so on, until the game unravels back to the first move. Selten called this logical but frustrating result the Chain-Store Paradox.

Reputation does not really enter the picture until we introduce incomplete information and the existence of (at least) two types of incumbents: tough ones who have payoffs that will always lead them to fight and weak ones who have the same payoffs as the incumbent in the previous example (see Kreps and Wilson 1982; Milgrom and Roberts 1982). As usual, the entrants know the distribution of incumbent types, but the type of a particular incumbent is private information. Now, even in the last round of a finite game a tough incumbent will fight and a weak entrant will stay out if the probability that she is facing a tough incumbent is high enough.

This changes the complexion of the game in a variety of ways. While a weak incumbent will still accommodate in the last period n, it will not necessarily do so in period $n-1$, because it has consequences for the last entrant's assessment of its toughness. If the expected gains to be had by convincing the last entrant that it is tough and convincing the (weak) entrant to stay out are greater than the benefits to be had by accommodating, the weak incumbent will act tough. Whether it will or not depends on the initial distribution of types and the payoff functions. Fortunately for weak incumbents, when the number of tough entrants is small, the prior probability that the incumbent is tough need not be large to completely deter challenges by weak entrants if the game is played for many periods. This is so, not because a long time horizon increases the penalty an entrant pays for an unsuccessful challenge, but rather, because a long time horizon increases the benefits of reputation, so that any type of incumbent has a large incentive to act strong. Because a weak entrant knows this, it will stay out.

Alt, Calvert, and Humes (1988) use a variant of the Kreps and Wilson (1982) incomplete information "solution" to the Chain-Store Paradox to explore the relationship between reputation and hegemonic stability. Figure 2.3 depicts the first period of what they refer to as the hegemonic game. In the first period of the two-period game, ally 1 chooses between obeying the dictates of its far more powerful alliance leader (the hegemon) and challenging them. The hegemon then chooses to punish the ally or acquiesce. In period 2, a second ally who has observed what has taken place in period 1 faces the identical problem.

The locus of the incomplete information is the cost x_t to the hegemon of punishing the ally in a given period t, where $x_t = 1$ (costly) with probability w and $x_t = 0$ (cheap) with probability $1 - w$. The hegemon knows w but learns what the exact cost of x_t will be for a particular period only at the beginning of that period. Thus at the beginning of period t it knows the value of x_t but is uncertain about that of x_{t+1}. The allies' uncertainty is still greater. They do not know what w is, only its distribution.

Alt, Calvert, and Humes want us to think of the parameter w as representing the weakness of the hegemon. The greater its value, the higher the expected cost of punishment. The hegemon knows its relative weakness; the task of ally 2 is to infer it from its knowledge of (1) the underlying random variable W from which w is drawn by Nature and (2) the hegemon's behavior in the first period. Following Alt, Calvert, and Humes , we assume that W has a beta distribution with parameters α and β, which roughly corresponds to a Bayesian actor who, starting with a flat prior, has observed α instances of weak hegemons and β instances of strong hegemons in the past. As in the case of the incomplete information version of the chain store, the hegemon's strategy in the first period is shaped by the implications it will have for ally 2 in the second period.

In equilibrium, the hegemon always punishes the ally when $x_t = 0$ and never punishes in the second period if $x_2 = 1$. In the latter case, like the weak incumbent in the finite chain-store game with incomplete information, it has no need to preserve a reputation in the last period. What happens in the other cases depends on the values of the parameters b, α, and β. Note that the expected value of w, the probability that the hegemon's punishment is costly, is $\alpha/(\alpha + \beta)$ at the beginning of the game. If an instance occurred where the ally was sure that the hegemon was weak, the revised distribution would be beta with parameters $\alpha + 1$

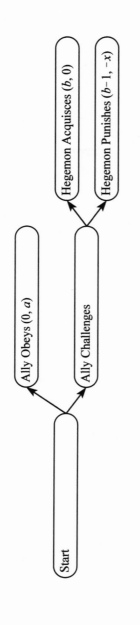

Figure 2.3: Hegemonic Game

and β, so that the expectation of W would be $(\alpha+1)/(\alpha+\beta+1)$. Similarly, if an instance occurred where the ally was sure that the hegemon was strong, the revised distribution would be beta with parameters α and $\beta+1$, so that the expectation of W would be $\alpha/(\alpha+\beta+1)$.

In a single play of the game, where changes in reputation play no role, an ally's expected value of challenging works out to $b - \beta/(\alpha+\beta)$; therefore an ally should challenge whenever $b > \beta/(\alpha+\beta)$. Alt, Calvert, and Humes describe four scenarios. In two of the cases, when $b \leq \beta/(\alpha+\beta)$, ally 1 is afraid to challenge and ally 2 has no reason to do otherwise. In the case where $b \geq (\beta+1)/(\alpha+\beta+1)$, both allies always enter; there is nothing that the hegemon can do to the first that will dissuade the second from challenging.

Only what they refer to as the third case, where $\beta/(\alpha+\beta) \leq b \leq (\beta+1)/(\alpha+\beta+1)$, involves reputation building. In this case, Alt, Calvert, and Humes derive an equilibrium in which the hegemon always punishes a challenge from ally 1 when $x_1 = 0$ and punishes with probability r when $x_1 = 1$, where

$$r = \frac{\beta\{1 - [b(\alpha+\beta+1) - \beta]\}}{\alpha[b(\alpha+\beta+1) - \beta]}.$$

This is chosen so as to be the optimal value of r that overcomes ally 2's incentive to challenge, if ally 2 observes the hegemon punishing ally 1.

In this case, ally 2 can potentially be deterred, but not by punishing always ($r = 1$). If the chance of punishing when $x_t = 1$ is r, then the larger r is, the less the act of punishing contributes to convincing ally 2 that x_t was actually 0, and therefore the less it lowers ally 2's estimate of w, which is the chance that ally 2 will successfully challenge. Thus, punishing with probability 1 will not deter ally 2. But never punishing is also not good, since it forfeits the opportunity of gain when $x_t = 1$. Thus, the hegemon needs to use the maximal value of r that will deter ally 2. Note that if the hegemon randomizes and the choice comes up to acquiesce, then ally 2 will always challenge. If the choice comes up to punish, then the critical value of r to deter ally 2 is

$$b = \frac{\beta(r\alpha + \beta + 1)}{(\alpha+\beta+1)(r\alpha+\beta)}$$

$$b(\alpha+\beta+1)(r\alpha+\beta) = \beta(r\alpha+\beta+1)$$

$$r = \frac{\beta[1+\beta-b(\alpha+\beta+1)]}{\alpha[\beta-b(\alpha+\beta+1)]}.$$

If the hegemon uses a value of r that is ϵ smaller than this number, ally

2 will always obey, so we assume that that is the action taken by ally 2 in equilibrium.

All of this occurs only if the hegemon responds to a challenge by punishment. If there is no challenge, there can be no punishment, and the value of w cannot be revised. Under this case, ally 2 will always challenge. A challenge by ally 1 occurs only when

$$b \ \leq \ \frac{r\alpha + \beta}{\alpha + \beta}.$$

This generates the Alt, Calvert, and Humes cases 3a and 3b.

In case 3, a partially separating equilibrium occurs, because weak and strong hegemons behave the same, but only a fraction of the time. Case 2 is a pooling equilibrium, because the hegemon always punishes ally 1 if challenged, regardless of the value of x_t. Case 4, where ally 2 can never be deterred, is a separating equilibrium, where the different hegemon types behave differently when challenged.

The Alt, Calvert, and Humes hegemonic game provides a useful vehicle for demonstrating the central role that separating, pooling, and semiseparating equilibria play in the assessment of reputation, but it also introduces a number of other themes that run through this book. One is that the analysis of even very simple games can rapidly become a complicated business. Even though the Alt, Calvert, and Humes model uses a two-period game to characterize what is, in reality, a repeated game, and ignores the almost inevitable event that the hegemon is uncertain about the strength of its challengers, we quickly find ourselves in the complex world of beta distributions, multiple equilibria, and mixed strategies. This should not surprise us. If such analyses were transparent, metaphors would serve as well as models.

The second theme is that the complicated mathematics necessary to analyze imperfect and incomplete information models can yield important substantive results. With all of its limitations, the vision of reputation that emerges from Alt, Calvert, and Humes is a far cry from what critics of realism and rational choice believe is a "naive" and noncontingent model of reputation. The following are some of the many implications of the article:

1. Hegemons are not always threatened by uncertainty about their strength.

2. Declining or weak hegemons are often deferred to by other states, not because those states mistake them for strong ones, but because

they know the hegemons have an incentive to act as if they were strong.

3. A state's reputation does not necessarily increase with a display of strength, because it is understood that weak states sometimes have an incentive to act as if they are strong.

4. No state will have to defend its reputation in all situations.

2.3 Principal-Agent Models

The second category of model is designed to deal with principal-agent relations. These represent situations that are shaped in an important way by asymmetric information (i.e., where one of the players knows something that the other does not) and by potential goal diversity. In the archetypical case, a supervisor (the principal) is faced with the problem of devising an effective method to prevent an employee (the agent) from shirking on the job. The problem is that the supervisor cannot observe the worker's effort directly and has reason to believe that it can be estimated only imperfectly by reliance on some surrogate measure (e.g., output) because that indicator is affected by other factors (e.g., machine breakdowns, other workers' efforts). This imperfect connection between effort and the measured outcome constitutes the locus of the uncertainty. The task of the principal is to design either some incentive scheme (an optimal contract) that gets the agent to internalize the consequences of her effort or some reliable technique (a mechanism) that can distinguish between high- and low-effort workers before they are hired.

The shop floor might appear to be a context far removed from those of interest to international relations specialists, but it is not. The problem of how states cope with asymmetric information and goal diversity similarly becomes increasingly salient as the field moves away from the unitary actor assumption and increases its efforts to understand the role of domestic politics. Certainly, there are countless instances where an agent who might have preferences that differ from those of the principal is charged with representing the latter's interest and either possesses or is given access to information that the principal does not share. This can occur whenever a population or group of individuals selects a leader, when a government appoints an ambassador or relies on expert judgment from some outside party, or when some part of the bureaucracy lets a contract to a private firm.

We illustrate the principal-agent model with an example adapted from Morrow (1991). This involves a principal—the electorate—and an

agent—the executive. The executive, acting as the state's agent, nego-
tiates an agreement with another state. If there is no monitoring, the
executive may act on behalf of his or her own interests, which do not
necessarily coincide with the national interest (identified here with the
interest of the electorate). However, there is a striking information asymmetry in that the executive is in possession of important information,
without which his or her performance in negotiating the treaty cannot
be evaluated. However, the electorate has an election sanction that,
properly used, can mitigate the deleterious effects of the information
asymmetry.

To begin the modeling effort, we specify the treaty negotiation model.
The treaty will be abstracted by a value $x \in [0, 1]$, in which the given
state (A) prefers higher values of x and the other state (B) prefers lower
values. The negotiation process consists of the executive of state A
proposing a value x, which state B either accepts or rejects. Since x
is state A's utility for the treaty and 0 is the utility of no treaty, A's
reservation price is also 0. The executive E has utility x for the treaty
and r $(0 \le r \le 1)$ for no treaty, so that r is E's reservation value. State
B's reservation value v is unknown to A (both the electorate and the
executive), with prior distribution that is uniform on $[0, 1]$. Thus, for
fixed x, the probability that B will accept the treaty is $1 - x$.

Without an agency problem, A could calculate the expected utility
from offering x. A's utility is x when $x < v$, so that B accepts the
treaty (probability $1 - x$), and 0 when $x > v$, so that B rejects the
treaty (probability x). The expected utility is then $x(1 - x)$, which is
maximized when $x = 1/2$; that is, A should offer a treaty that is midway
between the maximum treaty and the minimum treaty. However, E's
utility is x when $x < v$ (probability $1 - x$) and r when $x > v$ (probability
x). E's expected utility is then $x(1 - x) + rx$, which is maximized when
$x = (r+1)/2$; that is, E should offer a treaty that is midway between the
maximum treaty and E's reservation value. E has a larger reservation
value than A because a marginally beneficial treaty would be difficult to
pass in the legislature and would require extra effort (r) from E.

Now suppose that the reelection is worth w to the executive and that
$w > 1$. For the sake of simplicity, assume that w is common knowledge.
If A can observe the offer x, then there is an equilibrium in which A's
optimal outcome is obtained. A threatens E with loss of office unless E
offers the treaty $x = 1/2$, which is a sufficient incentive for E always to
behave properly in equilibrium.

But the electorate A may have poorer information about the value of the treaty than does the executive E, which introduces an information asymmetry. We can model this by having x be unobservable to A at the time the reelection decision needs to be made; A only observes whether the treaty was achieved or not. This reintroduces the likelihood that the executive will choose the offer $(r+1)/2$ that is optimal for the executive's own utility, rather than the offer $1/2$, which is optimal for the electorate's utility. The incentives are thus for the executive E to make an offer that is $r/2$ too large, which reduces the chance of achieving a treaty with B.

We add one additional feature to the model, a domestic economic factor. Let the economic conditions obtaining at the end of the game be e, where e is a normally distributed random variable with mean θ and standard deviation z, and where θ and z are common knowledge.

A must provide some incentive to keep the executive behaving properly, or at least more properly than without the incentive. Suppose this takes the form of two decision levels K_T and K_N, with $K_N > K_T$, where A reelects the executive if either (1) a treaty is signed and $e > K_T$ or (2) a treaty is not signed and $e > K_N$. Since $K_N > K_T$, this provides some additional incentive for E to choose to make a treaty.

Now E's utility must take into account four outcomes, all of which depend on x: whether B accepts the treaty or not; whether e is high enough to insure reelection. The overall utility for E is

$$(w+x)(1-x)(1-\Phi(K_T/z)) \quad + \quad (w+r)x(1-\Phi(K_N/z))$$
$$+ \, x(1-x)\Phi(K_T/z) \quad + \quad rx\Phi(K_N/z).$$

The first-order condition for the optimal choice of x is

$$\begin{aligned} 0 \quad = \quad & -2x(1-\Phi(K_T/z)) + (x-w)(1-\Phi(K_T/z)) \\ & + (w+r)(1-\Phi(K_N/z)) - 2x\Phi(K_T/z) \\ & + x\Phi(K_T/z) + r\Phi(K_N/z) \\ = \quad & 1 - 2x + r + w(\Phi(K_T/z) - \Phi(K_N/z)), \end{aligned}$$

so that E's optimal choice is

$$x = [1 + r - w(\Phi(K_T/z) - \Phi(K_N/z))]/2.$$

The electorate A can choose K_T and K_N to force E's choice to be $1/2$, the same as the electorate would have chosen, by forcing

$$(\Phi(K_T/z) - \Phi(K_N/z)) = r/w,$$

which is achievable since necessarily $r/w \in [0,1]$ (because $0 \le r \le 1$ and $w > 1$). Thus the electorate has a rule to force the executive to adhere to its own preferences.

In this simple model, there is a cost only to the executive, who may be booted out of office in spite of best efforts, but the only cost to the electorate is that they will remove from the executive position someone who did make the correct decision. There may be many more potential candidates to fill the office, so the cost may be small or nonexistent. More interesting agency problems (such as the one described in Chapter 3), result in the occurrence of *second-best outcomes*—strategies that are optimal given the information asymmetries, but which produce outcomes that are not as good as what could have been obtained with perfect information. Thus, another name for such second-best strategies might be optimal imperfection.

2.4   Trigger Strategies

Another important category of uncertainty is embedded in the imperfect quality of the observable information about the actions of another player. Here the difficulty lies not so much in determining the preferences of an opponent—often these are only too clear—but in estimating whether or not a defection or other behavior that we would like to respond to has actually taken place. This type of uncertainty exists more than one might imagine at the close of the twentieth century, and it is especially common in the security area. Despite impressive surveillance capability (and sometimes because of it), the United States has been uncertain about such things as the nuclear capability of North Korea, the character and volume of Chinese arm sales, the missile technology available to Iraq, and both the number and capabilities of troops under the control of Somali warlords.

Imperfect information causes problems because there are costs associated both with punishing a state for something that it did not do and with failing to punish it when it is appropriate to do so. To punish a state because of a false alarm or to punish it for a larger breach than it is actually guilty of is to forgo the gains of cooperation needlessly and invite retaliation. To withhold a penalty when it is due is to encourage future and possibly larger defections.

Trigger strategies are designed to deal with this sort of situation. Although the technical details are complicated, the basic logic is not difficult to understand. Suppose the State Department is in the process of designing a policy to deal with violations of a treaty dealing with the transfer of missile technology. It needs to decide what penalty to impose and when to impose it. It has to come up with a set of ten indicators that are associated with the execution of the proscribed technology transfer. No single indicator is conclusive: each carries with it an increased *probability* that the transfer has been executed. Because we are dealing with probabilities, a false positive or negative is always possible, and both types of errors are bound to occur over the long run.

Uncertainty makes the State Department's task difficult. In a world of perfect information, the decision about when to apply punishment is taken care of automatically—although in equilibrium it will never be applied—and the amount of punishment that must be threatened is modest: any level that will offset the benefit that the arms purveyor derives from the transfer will do. Under information uncertainty, things are more complicated. The decisions of how much and when to punish both require balancing the cost of the punishment, the benefit of deterring an arms transfer, and the accuracy of the indicators. The question then is how to determine the balance.

The joint specification of when and how much (or how long) to punish is a trigger strategy. The concept comes from Friedman (1971) and Green and Porter (1984) and the development of "optimal" trigger strategies is credited to Porter (1983). Our account owes much to these papers, although many of our techniques and conclusions differ from theirs. The use of trigger strategies for arms control was introduced in Downs and Rocke (1990).

We will present the ideas first in the context of an oligopoly of N risk-neutral oil-producing states. Each period, state i chooses a production level q_{it}, so that the total production is $Q_t = \sum q_{it}$. We denote the entire vector $(q_1, q_2, \ldots, q_N)$ by $\boldsymbol{q}_t$. Assume that the inverse demand function is $P(Q) = a - bQ$ and that the market price $\hat{p}$ is determined by the demand and a multiplicative stochastic component θ, so that $\hat{p} = P(Q)\theta$. Assume that θ has distribution $F()$ with density $f()$ and mean μ. Assume that the states face identical cost functions $C(q) = c_0 + c_1 q$ (this is not really necessary, but it allows direct calculation of solutions that are otherwise only defined implicitly). To avoid anomalies, we will make such assumptions as are necessary about the values of the parameters. For example, we need the marginal cost of producing an item to be less than the price at zero quantity (which is as high as the price gets); otherwise no production occurs at all. Formally, this is $0 < c_1 < \mu a$.

The basic idea of the *trigger price strategy* is that a price $\tilde{p}$ is set, and if the observed price $\hat{p}$ falls below this level, then one concludes that someone has broken the agreement. As a disincentive to breaking the agreement, everyone in the cartel agrees to defect to the Cournot quantity s for $T-1$ periods whenever the price is observed to fall below the trigger price $\tilde{p}$. Obviously, the trigger price needs to be carefully chosen so that any incremental gains from cheating (by producing more than the agreed amount) are at least balanced by the collective punishment that occurs when all of the states revert to the Cournot equilibrium. To accomplish this, a trigger price strategy needs to be able to deter two types of defection. First is defection by one state to its optimal one-period response (with the expectation that Cournot reversion would follow). This we call *gross defection*. Second is cheating by a small amount in the hopes that the trigger price threshold will not be passed—we call this *infinitesimal defection*.

Now it is easily calculated that state i has expected profit function

$$\pi_i(\boldsymbol{q}) = [A - BQ]q_i - c_0$$

where $A = \mu a - c_1$ and $B = \mu b$. In the absence of any agreement, the optimal choice of production level for state i given the production levels of the other states is found by solving the first-order condition

$$\frac{\partial \pi_i(\boldsymbol{q})}{\partial q_i} = A - BQ - Bq_i = 0$$

or

$$q_i = \frac{A - BQ_{(i)}}{2B}$$

where $Q_{(i)} = Q - q_i$. Since the states are identical, the simultaneous solution of all such conditions leads to some identical production s for each state, so that $Q = Ns$ and $Q_{(i)} = (N-1)s$. This leads to

$$s = \frac{A}{B(N+1)},$$

with a profit of

$$\pi_i(\boldsymbol{s}) = \frac{A^2}{B(N+1)^2} - c_0$$

per state. This is the Cournot equilibrium amount, and it represents the expected outcome if no collusion exists among the potential oligopolists. The hope of the oligopolists is to restrict total production, so that the aggregate revenues are increased.

If it were possible to come to an enforceable agreement, the oligopoly could require each state to produce an amount such that the total revenues to the oligopoly would be maximized. The total revenue is $\Pi = AQ - BQ^2 - Nc_0$, which is maximized when $A - 2BQ = 0$ or $Q = A/2B$. If divided equally among the participants, this leads to production vector r with identical components

$$r = \frac{A}{2BN}.$$

For a duopoly, this represents a 25 percent cut in production, and for large N this represents almost a 50 percent cut. The profit per state associated with this monopoly-level production is

$$\frac{A^2}{4BN} - c_0$$

and it is easily shown that this is greater than the profit from the Cournot equilibrium for any $N > 1$.

The task facing the oligopoly is to produce a self-enforcing agreement to restrict production to a level below that of the Cournot equilibrium. It may be that achievement of monopoly profits is not possible, but some improvement from the Cournot levels can perhaps be gained. Suppose that an agreement was made for each state to produce an amount $\tilde{q}$ which satisfies $r \leq \tilde{q} < s$. Suppose that the actual production is not observed, but only the market price $\hat{p}$ resulting from the total (unobserved) production Q. If everyone adheres to the agreement, the price will be $P(\tilde{Q})\theta$, which has expectation $P(\tilde{Q})\mu$. If the price falls much below this, then that is evidence that someone has violated the agreement.

Consider defection to the optimal response level. If all other firms are producing at the agreed-upon level of $\tilde{q}$, then the profit of state i is

$$\pi_i(\boldsymbol{q}) = [A - B(N - 1)\tilde{q} - Bq_i]q_i - c_0$$

so that the first-order condition is

$$\pi_i'(\boldsymbol{q}) = A - B(N - 1)\tilde{q} - 2Bq_i = 0$$

or

$$q_i = \frac{A - B(N - 1)\tilde{q}}{2B}$$

which differs from $\tilde{q}$ since $\tilde{q} < s$. Thus defection results in a one-period gain for state i. This is balanced by a $T-1$ period loss of the difference of the cooperative profit and the Cournot profit. The following can easily be seen:

1. For deterrence to be possible, the discount factor must not be too far from 1 (the discount rate must not be too large).

2. For a given value of T, there is a minimum production level to which the states can be held, corresponding to deterring defection with zero discount rate; this restricts possible equilibria.

3. Different values of T lead to different possible cooperative levels. Raising T makes more cooperative equilibria possible, but it also raises the cost of punishment.

Take as a numerical illustration (with arbitrary units) the case where the demand function is $P(Q) = 100 - .5Q$, the cost function of each state is $c(q) = 20 + q$, the random disturbance is lognormal, being the exponential of a normal variate with mean 0.5 and standard deviation 1, so that the mean is 1. Suppose that the discount factor is 0.9 and the number of periods of defection is 1. Finally, suppose that there are five states in the cartel.

In the Cournot equilibrium, each state produces 33 units, for a total of 165 units, yielding a price of 17.50 and a profit per state of 524.5. The monopoly solution is for each state to produce 19.8, for a total of 99 units, yielding a price of 50.5, and a per firm profit of 960.1. However, the monopoly quantity cannot be enforced by a trigger price strategy with a punishment period of 1. This is because a one-period defection producing 59.4 yields a price of 30.7 and a profit for the defecting firm of 1,774.18, and the profit from defection of 784.08 is too large to be overcome by one period of loss of $960 - 524.5 = 435.5$. However, a longer punishment period would be sufficient here. For example, four periods of defection, even discounted by 0.9 per period, is large enough to deter defection to the myopically optimal level.

The second kind of misbehavior that needs to be deterred is cheating by a small amount. For fixed T, the deterrent to cheating depends on the cooperative equilibrium that one is trying to attain $(\tilde{q})$ and on the trigger price $(\tilde{p})$. Consider the overall value of the game to player i as a function of the quantities chosen for fixed trigger price $\tilde{p}$ and reversion period $T - 1$. We have

$$
\begin{aligned}
V_i(\boldsymbol{q}) \;=\; & \pi_i(\boldsymbol{q}) + \Pr(\tilde{p} > \theta P(Q))\delta V_i(\boldsymbol{q}) \\
& + \Pr(\tilde{p} \le \theta P(Q)) \left[\sum_{\tau=1}^{T-1} \delta^\tau \pi_i(\boldsymbol{s}) + \delta^T V_i(\boldsymbol{q}) \right].
\end{aligned}
$$

Now let

$$
\begin{aligned}
\eta &= \Pr(\tilde{p} > \theta P(Q)) \\
&= \Pr(\theta < \tilde{p}/P(Q)) \\
&= F(\tilde{p}/P(Q)).
\end{aligned}
$$

Then

$$
\begin{aligned}
V_i(\boldsymbol{q}) &= \frac{\pi_i(\boldsymbol{q}) + (1 - \eta)\pi_i(\boldsymbol{s})(\delta - \delta^T)/(1 - \delta)}{1 - \delta^T - \eta(\delta - \delta^T)} \\
&= \frac{\pi_i(\boldsymbol{s})}{1 - \delta} + \frac{\pi_i(\boldsymbol{q}) - \pi_i(\boldsymbol{s})}{1 - \delta^T - \eta(\delta - \delta^T)}.
\end{aligned}
$$

This last formula shows that the value of the game is the value of the Cournot equilibrium, plus an appropriately discounted difference between the cooperative equilibrium and the Cournot equilibrium.

For this to be an equilibrium, it must be the case that state i has no incentive to change its production quantity at any time. We will examine this condition using the numerical example introduced above. Figure 2.4 shows the incentive to cheat a small amount for the above example cartel when they are trying to maintain a quantity of 25, which is somewhat larger than the monopoly share of 19.8, but not near the Cournot value of 33. The incentive varies with the trigger price, but no price gives an actual disincentive, so that the equilibrium cannot be maintained (for $T = 4$). Figure 2.5 shows the same sort of plot for a quantity of 30. Any trigger price between about 11 and 70 gives a negative incentive to raising the quantity. If a stable equilibrium is being sought, this occurs only at the points at which the axis is crossed; the trigger price would thus be 11.00.

It might be more profitable if a quantity nearer the monopoly quantity could be sustained. We have seen that $q = 30$ can be maintained by the trigger price strategy, because the axis is crossed, whereas $q = 25$ cannot. Clearly, there is a critical level of q that is the lowest that can be sustained. For these parameter values, that critical quantity is 26.604. Figure 2.6 shows the disincentive curve for this case, showing that a trigger price of about 35 will serve to maintain this equilibrium.

Now we can derive for each T the optimal quantity and trigger price and then compare the value of the resulting equilibrium. Often, for example with the lognormal errors we assume here, the optimal value of T is $T = \infty$ (Porter 1983).

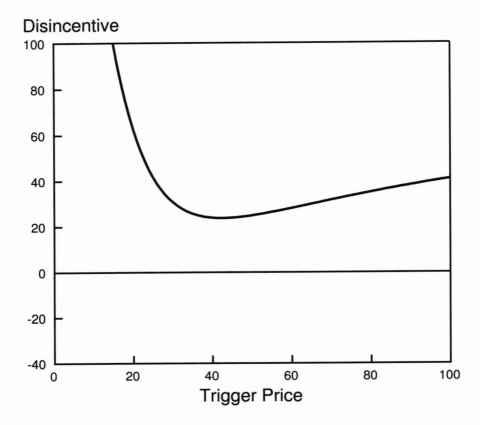

Figure 2.4: Disincentive to Defect for Different Triggers with $q = 25$

Disincentive

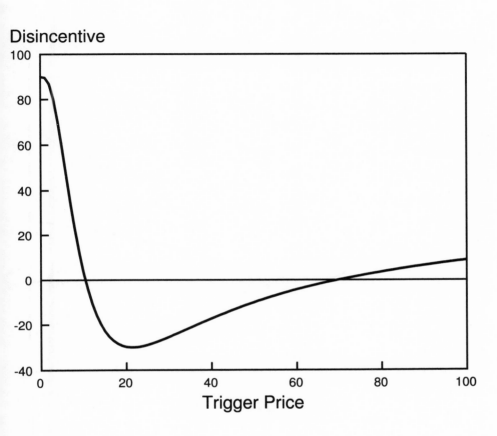

Figure 2.5: Disincentive to Defect for Different Triggers with $q = 30$

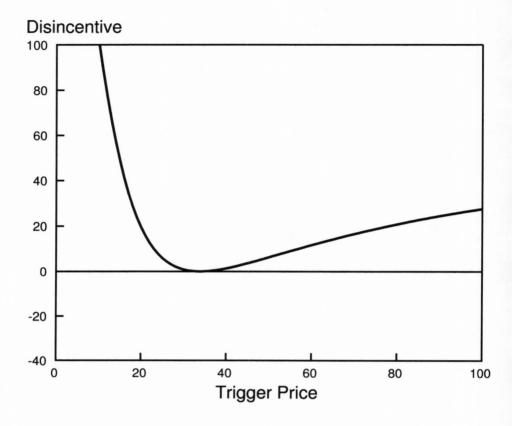

Figure 2.6: Disincentive to Defect for Different Triggers with $q = 26.604$

A finite value of T would be more comforting in several respects because it produces the empirically observed behavior of alternating periods of cooperation and intense competition (Green and Porter 1984). The finite T outcome is attractive enough apparently to cause Porter (1983) to make some fairly heroic assumptions about the random disturbance so that this would occur. The main line of the Porter paper assumes that the density of θ is increasing on its support, which is a very unusual property for a positive random variable. This would imply that there is a hard upper limit L on the size of the error and that this upper limit is also the most probable value. This is not a pattern frequently found in the analysis of data. With the more plausible lognormality assumption, $T = \infty$ is the optimal choice.

Since the time of Porter's paper, developments in game theory have given the modeler another tack for constructing optimal models with finite T. Consider the optimal trigger price strategy in which $T = \infty$, so that defection to the Cournot equilibrium, when it occurs, is forever. Ex ante, this is optimal. Furthermore, it is a Nash equilibrium because not one firm has an incentive to defect either from the original cooperative state or from the Cournot reversion. However, all firms must know that the Cournot reversionary state is not a Pareto optimal continuation. If all could agree to return to cooperation, all would be better off. So perhaps all would do so. But then the threat to defect forever is an empty one, since the Cournot reversion would itself fall apart.

Clearly, the punishment period must be long enough to deter a one-period defection—longer punishment periods may be disallowed under the concept of *renegotiation proofness*, which we discuss in Chapter 4. The concept of "renegotiation proofness" places a limit on what ever larger punishments can accomplish. It has a number of technical definitions, all involving the dimension of credibility that springs from assessments of a state's motivation rather than simply its capacity to carry out a particular threat. Assume that our group of oil producing states have learned the lesson that the level of cooperation that can be maintained in a mixed motive game is related to the level of punishment used to enforce it and that it agrees to punish overproduction by any one state by jointly abrogating the treaty forever. Suppose that by some unexpected sequence of events (e.g., the leader of one of the states faces a recession that threatens to destabilize her regime) one state violates the treaty. In response, the other state declare their production agreement null and void and resume production at the level that existed before the agreement was signed. After a significant time period has passed, the president of the state that violated the treaty communicates to the other state leaders that while she appreciates their mutual pledge to defect forever in the face of a violation, returning to unrestricted competition has already cost her more than what she gained by breaking the treaty. "I and my state have paid the price for our mistake. To continue producing at the competitive level will hurt you as well as us. Let's (re)negotiate a return to restricted production." This is the logic of renegotiation. Whenever a punishment strategy is vulnerable to such an offer, it is said not to be renegotiation proof. As a practical matter, think of it as restricting the credibility of punishment to a level no greater than the benefit that the violator has obtained by cheating. For the parameter values in the above illustration, a punishment period of 2 is long enough to deter defection to the Cournot equilibrium level; anything longer is off limits as not being renegotiation proof.

One point that has implications for the use of a trigger strategy in maintaining international agreements is that the equilibria introduced so far are symmetric if the players are identical. This need not be the case. First a more subtle point: not all firms need to have the same values of $\tilde{p}$ and T, although our presentation, like that of the previous literature, assumes this to be the case. Certainly, in a duopoly both sides must have the same value of these parameters, since when one reverts to the Cournot production level, the other should also. However, in a larger cartel firms could be grouped so that some would defect for one period if one trigger were exceeded and others would not defect until the price fell to a lower trigger. Such equilibria certainly exist, although they are more difficult to describe and to calculate.

2.5   Conclusion

This chapter has provided a very summary account of how various types of uncertainty are handled by noncooperative game theory. Readers interested in international relations who would like to better understand the less familiar principal agent and trigger strategy models are urged to consult one of the texts listed at the beginning of the chapter. Fudenberg and Tirole (1991) possess the virtue of containing a good treatment of both types of model.

It is important to note that we have only scratched the surface both in terms of the varieties of uncertainty we have considered and the mathematical techniques that can be used to deal with them. The content of our presentation has been limited by the character of the situation we will be dealing with in the next three chapters. Those reader curious about what happens when, as will often be the case, more than one kind of uncertainty are present will encounter such a situation in Chapter 5. We thought it best to postpone discussion of this more complicated modeling issue until we encountered a substantive context that demanded it.

Chapter 3
Gambling for Resurrection

The bad end unhappily, the good unluckily. That is what tragedy means.
  —Tom Stoppard

3.1 Introduction

One of the major tasks facing the citizenry of any state is to create domestic institutions that motivate bureaucrats and elected officials to act in accordance with their interests. This principal-agent problem is particularly challenging in areas like foreign policy where a chief executive is almost certain to have access to information that is not available to his or her constituency and may have preferences that are different from those of the average constituent.[1] In a democracy the mechanisms that help deal with this ever-present problem range from a free press and legislative declaration of war to electoral defeat and impeachment. Autocracies, by contrast, have far fewer of these mechanisms, and at the extreme there may be nothing more than the costly option of armed rebellion.

In this chapter we first use a principal-agent model to explore how a constituency should employ the sanction of removing an executive from office to cope with the information advantages of an executive in the area of conflict initiation. Because this decision rule is constant over time,

---

[1] Although there seems to be something of a consensus in the literature about the existence of differences in the preferences for conflict on the part of constituencies and chief executives, there is no consensus about the direction of the difference. Those exposed to an autocratic system, like Thucydides and Kant, appear to believe that leaders frequently have more aggressive preferences than their subjects. Those, like Lippman (1955) and Kennan (1951), whose experience lies more in democracies, have argued the opposite. Our argument requires nothing more than the real possibility that a difference exists.

it is appropriately considered to be an institution in the same sense as any other stable solution to an agency problem such as a bureaucracy's compensation scheme or regularized reporting requirements. While constituencies have a variety of such mechanisms that they can employ to try to insure that chief executivess follow their preferences in the area of conflict initiation (e.g., requiring the legislature to declare war), there are good substantive reasons to believe that the election sanction is among the most important. First, while the costs of imposing it vary greatly across societies, it is usually thought to be the most widely available and effective means of controlling executive behavior. As expressed through the electoral option in democratic societies, it has been found to play an important role in shaping the foreign policy behavior of governments (Gaubatz 1991; Morrow 1991). Second, the removal of a chief executive by whatever means is likely to signal subsequent executives most clearly about the limits of citizen tolerance and the character of citizen preferences. The expectation created by this signal is a critical part of any agency solution. Third, removal is the option of last resort, to be employed when other mechanisms fail, for example, in circumstances where the chief executive has concealed information or has exceeded the bounds of due process.

The analysis suggests that high information uncertainty forces a citizenry to look to battlefield success or to the apparent consequences of inaction as the gauge of the extent to which an executive is acting in a manner that is consistent with its preferences. In particular, it calls for the removal of an executive who initiates—or actively perpetuates—a losing campaign. This sanction is invoked not as punishment for failure or out of confusion about the nature of sunk costs but rather as a deterrent to keep subsequent executives from exploiting their information advantage to engage in aggression when a fully informed citizenry would not. Of course, it has a downside. It is extremely difficult to distinguish incidents where a good decision has led to a bad outcome from a bad decision. As a consequence, it is inevitable that a system will be established where some percentage of chief executives will be removed from office—indeed, have to be removed to prevent excessive aggressiveness—despite the fact that they have acted in a fashion that was entirely consistent with the public interest.[2] Thus, for a "good,"

---

[2] In spite of the fact that uncertainty and private information should be less prevalent in domestic affairs than in the international arena, results of Alesina, Londregan, and Rosenthal (1993) suggest that this phenomenon occurs in the former area as well. They found that voters are apparently influenced by the actual outcome of economic

public-regarding executive, having access to private information is more
of a curse than a blessing.

Having described how the electoral sanction will be "institutionalized" to cope with this domestic uncertainty–driven agency problem, we
then explore how this solution resonates beyond state borders to affect
international relations. The effect is driven by how executives respond
to the removal sanction. Executives know that their information advantages will prompt the constituency to evaluate their performance on
the basis of outcome alone, but they also know that their liability is
limited—the worst thing that can happen to them if they lose a conflict is also the least thing that will happen to them. Together these
act to inspire executives to "gamble for resurrection" when things go
poorly, by escalating or extending the conflict beyond what the median
constituency member would desire.[3] The result is more intense and/or
longer conflicts than would exist in a world where domestic constituencies did not have to deal with uncertainty about executive motives.

We begin by constructing a simple model that represents in schematic
form a game between a constituency and the chief executive that com-
mences when a conflict opportunity arises. The executive possesses information about the probable benefits, costs, and outcome that the constituency is not privy to, and indeed may well remain ignorant of even
after the resolution of the crisis. The task of the constituency is to create a decision rule for the use of its removal sanction that will deter its
leader, to the extent possible, from misrepresenting the situation to initiate a conflict when an accurately informed constituency would want to

---

growth and not by the difference between a reasonable prediction of the outcome and
what occurred. One possible explanation of this is that voters use this sanction to
insure that manipulation of expectations cannot be used by the executive to make
herself or himself look good.

[3]This is different from the hidden information problem in the typical retrospective
voting model (see Persson and Tabellini 1990; Rogoff and Sibert 1988; Hibbs 1987;
and Norpoth, Lewis-Beck, and Lafay 1991). In that model, greater or lesser voter
concern for the economy might affect the incentive for elected officials to attempt
to signal their competence by artificially manipulating economic performance, but
the failure of the voters to employ a decision rule that distinguishes competent from
incompetent executives does not increase the chances that the next executive will act
incompetently. In the case of the conflict agency model, however, failure to punish
one executive will increase the likelihood that the subsequent executives will disre-
gard constituency preferences. In the domestic economy agency model, gambling for
resurrection behavior is not modeled at all, although arguably it should be. One can
easily imagine circumstances where an executive, competent or incompetent, who has
the misfortune to be caught in a poor economy will be tempted to gamble for resurrection by implementing high-payoff, low-probability policies (Hess and Orphanides
1994; Smith 1994).

avoid it or vice versa. Moreover, this decision rule should be constructed so that it does not distort the actions of an executive who would already be inclined to do as the constituency wanted.

The model is intentionally one dimensional in that it assumes that the constituency is preoccupied with insuring that the executive will act as the constituency itself would with respect to initiating a conflict. This is done to understand as completely as possible the effect of uncertainty on the exercise of the removal sanction. Obviously, to the extent that other issues are more important and success in other areas can compensate for failure in this area, the model will be incomplete.

3.2 The Theory

Assume that there is a situation that potentially calls for the initiation of conflict (e.g., an international crisis). The executive possesses information θ that predicts the outcome (the success or failure and the associated costs and benefits) more precisely than is generally known. This provides the executive with the opportunity to conceal or distort for private purposes (e.g., drawing attention away from domestic problems, imperial ambitions, extreme risk averseness) information that would affect the public estimate of the advisability of conflict. Conversely, the existence of θ provides the constituency with a motive to establish some incentive scheme to prevent this.

The sequence of events in the model begins with the arrival of the crisis. The public has a best estimate in the form of prior means for the outcome X (expressed in units of the public's utility), which results from war or peace. The executive then observes the private information θ that will, in general, shift the best guess (mean) of the future value of X and also lower the variance. Then the executive decides whether to initiate conflict, and the outcome is observed. Based on the outcome and a comparison with prior expectations, the public decides whether to remove the executive. The goal of the constituency side of the game is to devise rules for applying the sanction based on X that provide the executive with an incentive to behave as the public would if it too had observed θ.

Formally, we assume that dependence of the distribution of X on the parameters θ (the private information) and I (an indicator of whether conflict has been initiated) is in the form of location and scale shifts of a single underlying distribution F; that is,

$$F(x|\theta, I) = F\left(\frac{x - \mu_{\theta I}}{\sigma_I}\right)$$

where $\mu_{\theta 1}$ and $\mu_{\theta 0}$ are the means of X under war and peace, respectively, and where we suppose for simplicity that the variance is constant at σ_1^2 and σ_0^2, respectively. We will scale θ so that a positive θ indicates that conflict will have stochastically better outcomes than inaction and so that negative θ indicates that it will have worse outcomes. Specifically, we assume that

$$\mu_{01} = 0 \tag{3.1}$$

$$\mu_{00} = 0 \tag{3.2}$$

$$\frac{\partial \mu_{\theta 1}}{\partial \theta} > 0 \quad (\forall \theta) \tag{3.3}$$

$$\frac{\partial \mu_{\theta 0}}{\partial \theta} < 0 \quad (\forall \theta) \tag{3.4}$$

$$\sigma_1 > \sigma_0. \tag{3.5}$$

The first two conditions are merely a scaling effect, but the second two express the fact that the expected payoff to initiating conflict (inaction) is an increasing (decreasing) function of θ. The final condition just says that outcomes of war are less predictable, in the sense of having a higher variance, than are outcomes of inaction.

If the constituency knew θ, then it could use the replacement sanction to force the executive to adhere to its preferences by simply declaring beforehand that he or she must engage in conflict whenever a positive θ is observed and refrain from doing so otherwise. To the extent that the executive valued continuance in office more than the utility of engaging in the behavior that the constituency did not want, this strategy would be optimal. Unfortunately, under the more typical situation where the executive has θ as private information and there is uncertainty about the extent to which his or her preferences mirror those of the median constituency member, it is necessary to devise a good second-best strategy.

Let α be a parameter that describes the tendency of the executive toward overaggressiveness, which we will denote by the term *adventurism*, or toward overcautiousness, which we denote by *timidity*. Suppose that $\alpha = 0$ corresponds to the executive having the same preference structure as the constituency, with $\alpha > 0$ showing a preference for adventurism and $\alpha < 0$ showing a tendency toward timidity (compared with the constituency).[4] Thus, the executive maximizes

$$E(u(X; \alpha)|\theta = \theta_0, I) \tag{3.6}$$

over choices of $I = 0$ or 1.

The primary purpose of introducing a removal sanction is for the constituency to force the executive's behavior to move nearer its own preferences than would be the case without the sanction. In this model, the only item of information that the constituency can use to decide if the executive should be removed from office is the outcome X of the crisis that led to war or peace. Clearly, there is only one reasonable form this can take: if war has occurred and $X < E_1$, the executive is removed; if war has not occurred and $X < E_0$, then the executive is removed. The public is thus faced with having to choose the points E_0 and E_1 at which removal results.

The public might reasonably have three primary criteria to help determine good values of E_0 and E_1. First, if the executive is unduly adventuresome ($\alpha > 0$), then a disincentive to initiate conflict should be applied. This should cause the executive to switch from some decisions to initiate conflict that the public would consider incorrect to a decision that the public would consider correct. Second, if the executive is too timid ($\alpha < 0$), a disincentive to hold back should be applied. This should cause some incorrect decisions to hold back to be switched to correct ones. Finally, the incentives should preferably not ever cause what would have been a correct decision to be switched to an incorrect one.

Technically, it is easier to begin with the conditions that would be necessary to insure the third condition. If no correct decision should be turned into an incorrect one by the application of sanctions, it is necessary that a greater disincentive be applied to conflict initiation when $\theta < 0$ and that a greater disincentive to hold back be applied when $\theta > 0$. By continuity, it follows that there should be no incentive either way when $\theta = 0$, the value at which the public would be indifferent between war and peace (if θ were known). In particular, this means that an executive with the same preferences as the public ($\alpha = 0$) should have no decision changed by the potential imposition of sanctions. A sufficient

---

[4]The parameter α may index attitude toward risk, with negative α indicating a preference for low-variance outcomes. Alternatively, α may index an intrinsic value placed on initiating conflict by the executive. For what follows, this distinction is unimportant—it is only necessary that α index the degree to which the executive would initiate conflict when the public would prefer not to.

condition for this to occur is that when $\alpha = 0$ and $\theta = 0$, the executive is still indifferent between war and peace even considering the incentive effects of sanctions.

Since there is only one sanction of unvarying size (which we denote by $-Q$), the only way to insure incentive neutrality in this case is to require that the probability of imposing the sanction after initiating conflict is the same as the probability of imposing the sanction under inaction, when $\theta = 0$. Technically, if F is the distribution function of X, then this condition is

$$F(E_0|\theta = 0, I = 0) = F(E_1|\theta = 0, I = 1).$$

This implies that there is only one parameter p that the constituency may choose and that

$$
\begin{aligned}
E_0 &= F^{-1}(p|\theta = 0, I = 0) \\
E_1 &= F^{-1}(p|\theta = 0, I = 1).
\end{aligned}
$$

If we let $z_p = F^{-1}(p)$, then

$$
\begin{aligned}
E_0 &= \mu_{00} + \sigma_0 z_p \\
E_1 &= \mu_{01} + \sigma_1 z_p.
\end{aligned}
$$

This illustrates a specific difficulty facing the constituency in this problem. Whereas in a typical principal-agent model,[5] the principal can choose an action from a continuum (amount of compensation), here it has only a binary sanction. When a punishment is under consideration, the constituency cannot choose its intensity, since there is only one punishment available. Ex ante, this means that the parameter the constituency can choose is the probability that the sanction will be imposed.

To appreciate how the use of a sanction as described above is a deterrent to either excessive adventurism or excessive timidity, we can calculate what the critical level of θ is for initiating conflict both with and without the sanction. Without the sanction, the executive will initiate conflict whenever

$$\mathrm{E}(u(X;\alpha)|\theta, I = 1) - \mathrm{E}(u(X;\alpha)|\theta, I = 0) > 0 \qquad (3.7)$$

whereas with the sanction, the condition is

$$
\begin{aligned}
&(\mathrm{E}(u(X;\alpha)|\theta, I = 1) - QF(E_1|\theta, I = 1)) \\
&-(\mathrm{E}(u(X;\alpha)|\theta, I = 0) - QF(E_0|\theta, I = 0) > 0. \qquad (3.8)
\end{aligned}
$$

[5]See Fudenberg and Tirole (1991); Levinthal (1988); or Tirole (1990).

The left-hand side of (3.8) is less than the left-hand side of (3.7) by

$$QF(E_1|\theta, I = 1) - QF(E_0|\theta, I = 0).$$

When $\theta < 0$, so that the constituency prefers inaction, this quantity is positive (by (3.1)–(3.4)), so that a disincentive to initiating conflict is provided. Similarly, when $\theta > 0$, so that the constituency prefers conflict, a disincentive to inaction is provided.

The above analysis is valid for any value of p, which is the probability of applying the sanction at the indifference point $\theta = 0$. There still remains the issue of optimal choice of p from the constituency's point of view.[6] To see how this should be selected, we begin by examining the sequence of events in the game, as follows:

1. The constituency chooses p and therefore z_p.
2. The information θ is observed by the executive. Suppose that the ex ante distribution of θ is a known function $G()$.
3. The executive decides whether to initiate conflict. This depends on the type α of the executive, information θ, and the sanction variable p.
4. The constituency observes a utility value X, which depends on θ and the decision of the executive. It may also depend on a prior distribution $A()$ that the constituency has for the type of the executive.

The complexity and conditional nature of this sequence of events makes an exact, closed-form analysis difficult. One approach in dealing with it is to identify a plausible value of θ at which the constituency would wish to provide the maximum disincentive to intervention; we then use the optimal p for this value of θ. In this form the optimal p does not depend on α, since the election sanction is assumed to be a separable contribution to the utility of the executive. This does not amount to an advance assumption about what value of θ will occur. Rather, it provides a value of θ at which to standardize. This value of θ would correspond to a situation that might plausibly occur and in which war would be particularly disastrous. An alternative, which we explore in the appendix, is to make more complex demands on the model, which results in implicit rather than explicit solutions. There, we analyze the

----

[6]That is, optimal given the information constraints. Obviously, any policy formulated without benefit of all the information is second best; under the circumstances, this is the best that can be done.

case where the constituency has an (accurate) prior distribution on the values of α and θ

If $\theta > 0$, then the issue is to deter inaction, and if $\theta < 0$, then the issue is to deter conflict initiation by the executive. If we choose the optimal policy for the utility at expectation of θ, rather than the exact value, which is the optimal p for the expected utility at θ, then, for a given value of $\theta < 0$, the optimal choice is the one that maximizes

$$
\begin{aligned}
D(p,\theta) &= Q(F(E_1|\theta, I=1) - F(E_0|\theta, I=0)) \\
&= Q\left(F\left(\frac{E_1 - \mu_{\theta 1}}{\sigma_1}\right) - F\left(\frac{E_0 - \mu_{\theta 0}}{\sigma_0}\right)\right) \\
&= Q\left(F\left(\frac{\mu_{01} + \sigma_1 z_p - \mu_{\theta 1}}{\sigma_1}\right) - F\left(\frac{\mu_{00} + \sigma_0 z_p - \mu_{\theta 0}}{\sigma_0}\right)\right) \\
&= Q\left(F\left(z_p + \frac{\mu_{01} - \mu_{\theta 1}}{\sigma_1}\right) - F\left(z_p + \frac{\mu_{00} - \mu_{\theta 0}}{\sigma_0}\right)\right).
\end{aligned}
$$

$$(3.9)$$

The first-order condition for the maximum value of D with respect to the choice of p is given by

$$
\begin{aligned}
0 &= f\left(z_p + \frac{\mu_{01} - \mu_{\theta 1}}{\sigma_1}\right) z_p' - f\left(z_p + \frac{\mu_{00} - \mu_{\theta 0}}{\sigma_0}\right) z_p' \\
0 &= f\left(z_p + \frac{\mu_{01} - \mu_{\theta 1}}{\sigma_1}\right) - f\left(z_p + \frac{\mu_{00} - \mu_{\theta 0}}{\sigma_0}\right)
\end{aligned}
$$

$$(3.10)$$

and the second-order condition is

$$
\begin{aligned}
0 &< f'\left(z_p + \frac{\mu_{01} - \mu_{\theta 1}}{\sigma_1}\right) (z_p')^2 - f'\left(z_p + \frac{\mu_{00} - \mu_{\theta 0}}{\sigma_0}\right) (z_p')^2 \\
&+ f\left(z_p + \frac{\mu_{01} - \mu_{\theta 1}}{\sigma_1}\right) z_p'' - f\left(z_p + \frac{\mu_{00} - \mu_{\theta 0}}{\sigma_0}\right) z_p''.
\end{aligned}
$$

$$(3.11)$$

Clearly, some conditions are required on F to guarantee the existence of a solution. The theorem below shows that sufficient conditions are that the density f is differentiable and strongly unimodal. This theorem shows that given a particular situation that is either likely or greatly feared, where the executive needs to be deterred from a particular act of adventurism (timidity), there is an optimal strategy. It is not possible optimally to deter undesired actions in all situations, so one particular type must be chosen as being likely to occur, or important to deter, and then the optimal policy for this case is used in general.

Proposition 3.1 *Let the standardized density f of X be differentiable and strongly unimodal. Then, for each fixed θ, there exists a unique solution to the constituency's maximization problem defined by (3.9).*

PROOF. Strongly unimodal means that there exists a unique point M such that $f(x)$ is strictly increasing for $x < M$ and strictly decreasing for $x > M$. Without loss of generality, we will take $\alpha > 0$ and $\theta < 0$; the other cases follow directly. In this case, $-a = (\mu_{01} - \mu_{\theta 1})/\sigma_1 < 0$ and $b = (\mu_{00} - \mu_{\theta 0})/\sigma_1 > 0$. Choose p so that $z_p + b = M$; then the first-order criterion is clearly negative. Choose p so that $z_p - a = M$; then the first-order criterion is clearly positive. By continuity, there exists a zero. Strong unimodality implies that there cannot be a second solution. If both $z_p - a$ and $z_p + b$ are on the same side of the mode, then the density values cannot be equal since the density is strictly decreasing (increasing). If they are on opposite sides of the mode, as is the case with the solution just derived, then the difference in the densities is clearly strictly increasing, so there cannot be another zero. The second-order condition (3.11), evaluated at the solution, becomes

$$f'\left(z_p + \frac{\mu_{01} - \mu_{\theta 1}}{\sigma_1}\right)(z'_p)^2 - f'\left(z_p + \frac{\mu_{00} - \mu_{\theta 0}}{\sigma_0}\right)(z'_p)^2$$

which is clearly positive (because $z_p - a$ and $z_p + b$ lie on opposite sides of the mode), showing that the critical point is a maximum. $\square$

Thus, given fairly weak conditions on the distribution of the uncertainty, an optimal strategy to deter any prechosen situation is available. Since this strategy differs depending on the situation it is intended to deter, it is not a complete solution. Nonetheless, if the standardizing situation is well chosen, this strategy will be a reasonable general choice.

As a specific mathematical illustration, suppose that the ex ante distribution of θ is normal with mean $-2\sigma_0$, so that the outcome would almost always favor inaction rather than war. Assume that $\mu_{\theta 1} = \theta$ and that $\mu_{\theta 0} = -\theta$ (this is a simple way to have θ indicate whether conflict initiation is desirable) and suppose that F is standard normal. Then the condition for optimality becomes

$$\left(z_p - \frac{\theta}{\sigma_1}\right)^2 = \left(z_p + \frac{\theta}{\sigma_0}\right)^2$$

$$-\frac{2z_p\theta}{\sigma_1} + \frac{\theta^2}{\sigma_1^2} = \frac{2z_p\theta}{\sigma_0} + \frac{\theta^2}{\sigma_0^2}$$

$$z_p = \frac{\theta^2(\sigma_1^{-2} - \sigma_0^{-2})}{2\theta(\sigma_1^{-1} + \sigma_0^{-1})}$$

$$= 0.5\theta(\sigma_1^{-1} - \sigma_0^{-1}). \qquad (3.12)$$

Standardizing at $\theta = -2\sigma_0$, one would use

$$z_p = -\sigma_0(\sigma_1^{-1} - \sigma_0^{-1})$$

$$= 1 - \frac{\sigma_0}{\sigma_1}.$$

If war had twice the standard deviation of inaction, then one would choose $z_p = .5$, so that $p = .5$, $E_0 = E_1 = 0$. Note that the assumption that war has a higher standard deviation is necessary here; otherwise all choices of p are equally preferable.

The closed-form solution (3.12) allows us easily to comment on the dependence of the solution on the parameters. Note that z_p is a linear function of the situation at which the punishment is to be standardized. As θ becomes more and more negative, so that war becomes more and more undesirable, the value of z_p rises, and the optimal percentage of the time that the sanction is applied also rises. The other critical variable is the ratio σ_1/σ_0 between the standard deviation of the result under war and the standard deviation under peace. The closer this is to 1, the less likely it is that the sanction will be applied.

Under information asymmetry, the bottom line from a qualitative standpoint is that a constituency that places a high value on having its wishes respected with regard to conflict initiation will key its use of the removal sanction to conflict outcomes. Ceteris paribus, the greater the information asymmetry and the worse the conflict outcome, the greater the removal rate of executives who are unsuccessful at war in comparison with the removal rate of executives who do not go to war.

Evidence that constituencies act in a fashion consistent with the model can be found in Bueno de Mesquita, Siverson, and Woller (1992). Using data from 1816–1975 that consist both of states that participated in wars and of those that did not, they find (1) that leaders who initiate and lose a costly war stand an 80 percent chance of being replaced and (2) that the probability of replacement increases with the severity of the defeat (measured in battle deaths).[7] Most of the regimes in

---

[7]Cases where the regime change was forced by an enemy were dropped from the analysis.

question were autocracies, where one would expect to find the greatest information asymmetries.[8]

Obviously, these findings are more suggestive than conclusive. A proponent of competency-based retrospective voting, for example, could argue that they indicate nothing more than an attempt to remove incompetent, rather than adventuresome, executives. While we think that competency assessment may well be playing a role, Bueno de Mesquita, Siverson, and Woller also found that leaders who initiated a losing war were removed from office at a higher rate than those who lost a war that they did not initiate. The argument that initiators are more adventuresome than noninitiators seems somewhat stronger than the argument that those who initiate losing wars are more incompetent than those who fail to prepare for them. Furthermore, a competency-based removal would not be necessary for executives who are not subject to reelection, since the cost of the executive's misestimation is sunk and cannot be recovered by punishment. Thus, our agency model seems to provide the best explanation. A further fit between our model and the results of Bueno de Mesquita, Siverson, and Woller is that our model predicts that the worse the outcome, the greater the likelihood of removal, since removal is optimally a function of how bad the outcome was and not just that it was bad.

3.3 The Executive's Dilemma

Second best solutions to agency problems are frequently costly from the perspective of both the agent and the principal. The irony here is that a cost is borne by executives who had the very preferences desired by the constituency, but whose misfortune it is to see their responsible decisions in difficult situations result in poor outcomes.

As we have seen, because the constituency cannot observe directly whether the executive has made the right decision, it must establish a set of punishments for poor outcomes or face losing the deterrent to future executives who might be tempted to act contrary to their interests. Unfortunately, the relationship between the quality of a decision and the character of the outcome is notoriously imperfect. Inevitably, a

[8]Not only democracies, then, but also most autocracies are vulnerable to the agency problem described here, since executives of autocratic states are, at least at some point, subject to forcible removal by an elite that functions in the role of the principal.

certain percentage of decisions that perfectly represent constituency desires ex ante lead to bad outcomes, and the executive responsible will be punished for no reason other than that he or she was unlucky and the constituency does not possess the information to distinguish bad luck from manipulation.

In this model the parameter p is the chance that an executive whose preferences perfectly mirror those of the constituency will be turned out of office if faced with a cusp decision where $\theta = 0$. The constituency must do this to deter executives with different objectives. This has the interesting implication that the worst thing that can happen to an executive is to be faced with a close decision. If the information θ clearly indicates a preferred alternative, then by acting as the public wishes the executive can act to reduce the chance of being expelled from office to far below p. If, however, the information θ is completely neutral, then whichever way the executive acts results in the (perhaps large) chance p of removal from office. Note that this is different from saying that close decisions are difficult to make. The assertion is that they are dangerous to the executive's political health, regardless of which of the two options is chosen.

3.4 Gambling for Resurrection

The model we have developed so far ignores two aspects of the real-world agency problem that have important implications. First, war is actually not a once-and-for-all decision; rather, it unfolds over time, with many opportunities to continue or reduce the level of conflict. Second, the sanction of removal from office cannot be applied instantaneously. In the United States the voters' sanction can be imposed only at fixed election times. Even in a parliamentary democracy there are inevitable time lags between a given event, public disapproval, the decision to call an election, and the election itself. Practical obstacles are even greater in autocracies. The period of time covered by the model should be thought of as the interval between the initiation of conflict and the first opportunity to remove the executive.

Consider the sequence of events if we divide the period of executive decision into two stages.

1. The executive obtains a piece of private information θ_1 that gives him or her improved estimates $\mu_{\theta_1 I_1 1}$ $(I_1 = 0, 1)$ of the average result of conflict or inaction in the first stage.

2. The first-stage outcome X_1 is observed by the executive and may or may not be observed by the constituency.

3. The executive obtains a second piece of private information θ_2 that gives the executive improved estimates $\mu_{\theta_2 I_2 2}$ $(I_2 = 0, 1)$ of the average added result of conflict or inaction in the second stage.

4. The second-stage outcome X_2 is observed by the executive and possibly the constituency. The total outcome (in units of the constituency's utility) is $X = X_1 + X_2$, which is observed by all.

5. The constituency decides whether the executive (or the party of the executive) should be kept in office based on the two decisions and on the overall outcome (and possibly on the individual stage outcomes, depending on what the constituency has been able to observe).

Assume that the constituency establishes two criterion levels for values of X that will result in the executive being removed: one for the case of a first-stage conflict initiation and one for the case of a first-stage inaction. An executive decides (correctly) to initiate conflict but is unlucky and has an unfavorable outcome that will result in removal from office unless the situation is improved. At this point, removal may be all but inevitable even if the executive makes peace, because the losses have already passed the removal threshold, and if peace has a low variance, the chance of raising the outcome sufficiently high to avoid loss of office is quite small. The alternative of escalation is attractive because the greater variance of conflict holds out a better possibility of rising above the threshold for staying in office, even though the expected value of the outcome may be lower than that of peace. The phenomenon that emerges from our model is sometimes called *gambling for resurrection*.

The main problem here is limited liability. Once the constituency seems determined to expel the executive from office for poor performance, it has no other sanction to apply. An executive, then, risks little in the way of further punishment by gambling, and if the gamble is successful, he or she may gain the right to stay in office .

It is important to appreciate the difference between the gambling for resurrection rationale for executive behavior in deteriorating situations such as the United States experience in Vietnam and standard explanations such as George Ball's infamous characterization of the "slippery slope."

Once we suffer large casualties, we will have started a well-nigh irreversible process. Our involvement will be so great that we cannot—without national humiliation—stop short of achieving our complete objectives. (Quoted in Staw and Ross 1989, 216)

Note that Ball envisions an entire nation struggling to avoid "national humiliation." The principal-agent approach, by contrast, encourages us to view unprofitable escalation as a strategy used by a head of state to avoid the punishment costs associated with a poor outcome. Yes, Ball's slippery slope exists, but it is a personal one with contours designed to avoid the loss of political power. The two explanations also lead to sharply different predictions about the behavior of the successor president(s). According to Ball's model, we would expect any successor elected before victory was ultimately achieved to be equally committed to carrying on with the war. Voters driven by national pride would demand it. On the other hand, our principal-agent model predicts otherwise—that the voters would do everything possible to elect a president who was committed to withdrawal.

In general, trying to distinguish gambling for resurrection from behavior that stems from nothing more than an executive carrying out the wishes of his or her constituency is no easy matter, but the modern history of unsuccessful interventions suggests that the agency explanation is important. The volume by Levite et al. (1992) contains case studies of the most prominent unsuccessful interventions of the past three decades. In the case of each democracy or quasi democracy (e.g., the United States in Vietnam, India in Sri Lanka, Israel in Lebanon, and South Africa in Angola), the government either continued to intervene or escalated the intensity of the conflict in the face of strong public opposition, just as the principal-agent model predicts.[9] Vietnam may be the archetypical example of this, but detailed descriptions of the situations in Lebanon, Sri Lanka, and South Africa leave the reader with an impression of interventions that continued after the median voter had come to believe that disengagement was the more sensible course. Moreover, a major part of the mandate of subsequent executives, those who took office after public antipathy to intervention had peaked, involved disengagement. Both of these developments are consistent with the principal-agent model; neither is what one would expect if an entire population was attempting to avoid national humiliation.

Gambling for resurrection as a motive for escalatory behavior is well known, but its connection to an institution designed to deter executives from exploiting their information advantage is not. Ellsberg (1972), for example, argued that the United States remained in Vietnam because no U.S. president could survive withdrawal; he never suggested that the

---

[9]There was similar public opposition to the Soviet Union's intervention in Afghanistan, but it is less clear who the constituency was in that case.

organizational demands of uncertainty and the bad luck "trap" were responsible for this tragic state of affairs. In part because he failed to connect the two processes, Ellsberg believed that a president could survive Vietnam by simply postponing total withdrawal. The principal-agent model tells us that this would not work. Once casualties reach a certain threshold, only victory can save the executive, not the mere avoidance of defeat. The distinction is important. Ceteris paribus, our model predicts that Vietnam would cost Johnson his reelection in 1968 election; Ellsberg's model suggests that it would not.

3.5 Conclusion

Uncertainty poses a serious problem for a constituency attempting to insure that its chief executive makes decisions that reflect its desires. This is particularly true in the area of foreign policy. Not only does the constituency have imperfect information about its executive's true preferences, but it also does not have access to the same quality information about the benefits and costs of different policies.

One prominent way for a constituency to cope with this problem is to institutionalize its removal sanction in such a way that both an overly passive and an overly aggressive executive is deterred from following his or her preferences. In the case of conflict decisions such as when to declare war and when to intervene, the typically large amount of uncertainty means that the constituency must base its decision to retain an executive on the outcome of conflict not on its ex ante advisability. If an executive loses, he or she must be replaced.

While this institutional strategy represents the best a constituency can do when uncertainty is very high, it not without costs. One is that a constituency will occasionally have to pay the price of removing a highly effective and innocent executive from office even though he or she made the best possible decision under the circumstances. This is necessary because uncertainty makes it impossible to know which executives acted in the best interests of the constituency and which were pursuing their own ends. The constituency could, of course, simply ask the executive whether defeat was the product of a good decision, but one does not have to be a game theorist to appreciate how self-interest would tend to make the answer uninterpretable. Like a defendant's plea that he was ignorant of the law, it may or may not be the case, but it is an excuse that all will plead.

The most important cost of this optimally imperfect solution is that it inspires executives to gamble for resurrection by continuing a conflict longer or escalating it to levels greater than a well-informed public would desire. Like the president of a failing savings and loan in the 1980s, the executive has nothing to lose by trying ever more risky strategies. Recent case studies of interventionist behavior in Vietnam, Sri Lanka, and elsewhere suggest that gambling for resurrection may be common and that it is the international by-product of a domestic institution, not the strategy of a constituency bent on salving its national pride.

One of the most interesting implications of the model involves the trade-off between two goals: removing executives from office to cope with the principal-agent problem, and minimizing gambling for resurrection. The more a constituency tries to limit future executive aggressiveness by increasing the punishment for poor outcomes, the more it creates an incentive for an executive who has initiated an unsuccessful war or intervention to continue the conflict, even though it would be terminated by a fully informed constituency. Conversely, the more a constituency seeks to mitigate this problem of gambling for resurrection by being sympathetic to an executive's argument that a war has gone badly for reasons that could not have been foreseen, the more the constituency will be led into conflicts that it would not have entered had it been fully informed.

The cost of confusing the two situations can obviously be very high. If a state thinks that it is suffering the effects of adventurism, when it is actually suffering the effects of gambling for resurrection—a real possibility given the lack of familiarity with the dynamics of the latter—it may move to increase the probability of removal for unsuccessful campaigns. This will further increase the incentive for gambling for resurrection, and the cure in effect will have made the disease worse. We cannot speak to how frequently this kind of problematic misspecification takes place, but its possibility suggests the merits of developing solutions to the agency problem that do not increase the incentive for gambling for resurrection, and vice versa. A free press is an example of the former; parliamentary democracy is an example of the latter, since it permits a more timely removal of an executive than do fixed elections.

3.6   Appendix: Optimal Bayesian Policies

We have in this chapter examined the case where the populace has no reliable prior distribution on the preferences α of the executive and the private information θ. In this appendix we consider the case where the populace does have such prior opinions about likely values of the private information variable θ (and thus a prior on the outcome itself) and about the type α of the executive. Suppose that the constituency's prior estimate of the value of the private information to be observed by the executive is given by $\theta = \xi + \tilde{\theta}\tau$, where ξ and τ are known constants (prior mean and standard deviation) and where the density $g()$ of $\tilde{\theta}$ has mean 0 and variance 1 (e.g., standard normal). Then the observed outcome X has a density h, which is a convolution of f and g as follows:

$$h(x|\xi, \tau, \mu_{\theta I}, \sigma_{\theta I}, I) = \int \sigma_I^{-1}\tau^{-1} f\left(\frac{x - \mu_{\theta I}}{\sigma_I}\right) g\left(\frac{\theta - \xi}{\tau}\right) d\theta$$

In the specific case in which F and G are standard normal and $\mu_{\theta I} = \pm\theta$, we have that x is normally distributed with mean ξ and variance $\sigma_I^2 + \tau^2$. Contrast this with the executive's prior on x after observing θ, which is normal with mean θ and variance σ_I^2. Thus, the executive's private information both gives a different estimate of the likely outcome and reduces the uncertainty, compared with the public's estimates.

Now the outcome that is observed depends on the executive's decision, which in turn depends on θ and α. First, consider the public-mirroring executive in which $\alpha = 0$. Then the decision to initiate conflict will be made exactly when $\theta > 0$. Consequently, the expected payoff to the public is

$$P_0 = \int_{-\infty}^{0} \int_{-\infty}^{\infty} x\sigma_0^{-1}\tau^{-1} f\left(\frac{x - \mu_{\theta 0}}{\sigma_0}\right) g\left(\frac{\theta - \xi}{\tau}\right) dx\, d\theta$$
$$+ \int_{0}^{\infty} \int_{-\infty}^{\infty} x\sigma_1^{-1}\tau^{-1} f\left(\frac{x - \mu_{\theta 1}}{\sigma_1}\right) g\left(\frac{\theta - \xi)}{\tau}\right) dx\, d\theta.$$

If $\alpha \neq 0$, then the value of θ that divides decisions to initiate conflict from decisions to abstain is not 0. Let $t_0(\alpha)$ be that value of θ satisfying

$$E(u(x; \alpha)|\theta = t_0(\alpha), I = 1) = E(u(x; \alpha)|\theta = t_0(\alpha), I = 0).$$

Then the payoff to the public from this executive's decision (with no sanction) is

$$P_\alpha = \int_{-\infty}^{t_0(\alpha)} \int_{-\infty}^{\infty} x\sigma_0^{-1}\tau^{-1} f\left(\frac{x - \mu_{\theta 0}}{\sigma_0}\right) g\left(\frac{\theta - \xi}{\tau}\right) dx\, d\theta$$
$$+ \int_{t_0(\alpha)}^{\infty} \int_{-\infty}^{\infty} x\sigma_1^{-1}\tau^{-1} f\left(\frac{x - \mu_{\theta 1}}{\sigma_1}\right) g\left(\frac{\theta - \xi}{\tau}\right) dx\, d\theta$$

which differs from the outcome of the ideal executive by

$$P_\alpha = \int_{t_0(\alpha)}^{0} \int_{-\infty}^{\infty} x\sigma_0^{-1}\tau^{-1} f\left(\frac{x - \mu_{\theta 0}}{\sigma_0}\right) g\left(\frac{\theta - \xi}{\tau}\right) dx\, d\theta$$

$$-\int_{t_0(\alpha)}^{0}\int_{-\infty}^{\infty} x\sigma_1^{-1}\tau^{-1}f\left(\frac{x-\mu_{\theta 1}}{\sigma_1}\right)g\left(\frac{\theta-\xi}{\tau}\right)dx\,d\theta$$

$$=\int_{t_0(\alpha)}^{0}\int_{-\infty}^{\infty} x\left(\sigma_0^{-1}f\left(\frac{x-\mu_{\theta 0}}{\sigma_0}\right)\right.$$

$$\left.-\sigma_1^{-1}f\left(\frac{x-\mu_{\theta 1}}{\sigma_0}\right)\right)\tau^{-1}g\left(\frac{\theta-\xi}{\tau}\right)dx\,d\theta$$

which is the cost of an executive who does not perfectly reflect the preferences of the constituency.

When a sanction is applied at z_p, the indifference point $t_Q(\alpha,p)$ of the executive is defined by the condition

$$\mathrm{E}(u(X;\alpha)|\theta=t_Q(\alpha,p),I=1)-QF(E_1|\theta=t_Q(\alpha,p),I=1)=$$
$$\mathrm{E}(u(X;\alpha)|\theta=t_Q(\alpha,p),I=0)-QF(E_0|\theta=t_Q(\alpha,p),I=0).$$
$$(3.13)$$

The payoff to the public from this option is

$$P_\alpha^Q = \int_{-\infty}^{t_Q(\alpha,p)}\int_{-\infty}^{\infty} x\sigma_0^{-1}\tau^{-1}f\left(\frac{x-\mu_{\theta 0}}{\sigma_0}\right)g\left(\frac{\theta-\xi}{\tau}\right)dx\,d\theta$$
$$+\int_{t_Q(\alpha,p)}^{\infty}\int_{-\infty}^{\infty} x\sigma_1^{-1}\tau^{-1}f\left(\frac{x-\mu_{\theta 1}}{\sigma_1}\right)g\left(\frac{\theta-\xi}{\tau}\right)dx\,d\theta$$

for fixed α and is

$$P^Q = \int\int_{-\infty}^{t_Q(\alpha,p)}\int_{-\infty}^{\infty} x\sigma_0^{-1}\tau^{-1}f\left(\frac{x-\mu_{\theta 0}}{\sigma_0}\right)g\left(\frac{\theta-\xi}{\tau}\right)A(\alpha)\,dx\,d\theta\,d\alpha$$
$$+\int\int_{t_Q(\alpha,p)}^{\infty}\int_{-\infty}^{\infty} x\sigma_1^{-1}\tau^{-1}f\left(\frac{x-\mu_{\theta 1}}{\sigma_1}\right)g\left(\frac{\theta-\xi}{\tau}\right)A(\alpha)\,dx\,d\theta\,d\alpha$$

when averaged over a prior distribution $A(\alpha)$ of α.

Now the first order condition for optimal choice of p is

$$0 = \int\frac{\partial t_Q(\alpha,p)}{\partial p}A(\alpha)\int_{-\infty}^{\infty} x\sigma_0^{-1}\tau^{-1}f\left(\frac{x-\mu_{\theta 0}}{\sigma_0}\right)g\left(\frac{\theta-\xi}{\tau}\right)dx\,d\alpha$$
$$-\int\frac{\partial t_Q(\alpha,p)}{\partial p}A(\alpha)\int_{-\infty}^{\infty} x\sigma_1^{-1}\tau^{-1}f\left(\frac{x-\mu_{\theta 1}}{\sigma_1}\right)g\left(\frac{\theta-\xi}{\tau}\right)dx\,d\alpha$$

where $\partial t_Q(\alpha,p)/\partial p$ is determined by implicit differentiation of (3.13) (note that E_0 and E_1 depend on p as does $t_Q(\alpha,p)$). The second-order condition is

$$0 < \int\frac{\partial^2 t_Q(\alpha,p)}{\partial p^2}A(\alpha)\int_{-\infty}^{\infty} x\sigma_0^{-1}\tau^{-1}f\left(\frac{x-\mu_{\theta 0}}{\sigma_0}\right)g\left(\frac{\theta-\xi}{\tau}\right)dx\,d\alpha$$

$$- \int \frac{\partial^2 t_Q(\alpha, p)}{\partial p^2} A(\alpha) \int_{-\infty}^{\infty} x \sigma_1^{-1} \tau^{-1} f\left(\frac{x - \mu_{\theta 1}}{\sigma_1}\right) g\left(\frac{\theta - \xi}{\tau}\right) dx \, d\alpha$$

This strategy would clearly be more difficult to implement than the one described in this chapter. It does, however, provide a yardstick against which more feasible strategies can be measured.

Chapter 4
Optimal Imperfection: GATT and the
Uncertainty of Interest Group Demands

A community is infinitely more brutalized by the habitual employment
of punishment than it is by the occasional occurrence of crime.
—Oscar Wilde

4.1   Introduction

In the absence of effective third-party enforcement, the task of maintaining cooperation depends on the expectations that states establish about
how they will respond to violations. Quite often these expectations come
to be explicit features of the norms of regimes, the rules and procedures
of international organizations, treaty provisions, and even the domestic
laws of the constituent states. This chapter explains how uncertainty
about interest group demands—as well as the demands themselves—can
determine the character of such institutional rules.

The role of domestic interest groups in instigating treaty violations
and in reshaping the character of cooperation is, of course, well doc-
umented. This is particularly true in the area of trade. Agricultural
and industrial trade groups haunt the legislative chambers of the industrial world arguing for special tariffs and subsidies. In the United
States legislators from agricultural states—regardless of party loyalty
or ideological stance on other issues—are wildly enthusiastic about any
and every barrier to foreign-produced agricultural products and simultaneously indiscriminate in their embrace of every kind of subsidy for
their own goods. Representatives of states with notable auto, shoe, or

textile industries behave similarly. This pattern is repeated throughout the developed world (Hillman 1989).

If these interest group demands exist when a trade agreement is being negotiated and the political benefits of responding to them are sufficiently great, they can be dealt with by creating exceptions, such as those covering agriculture products in the GATT. Yet what about the possibility that the ecology of protectionist demands will change after an agreement is already in place? This is not unusual. New products emerge, recessions occur, and administrations find themselves in need of new electoral and financial resources. While one can imagine a state regularly renegotiating its trade agreements in response to such contingencies, the transaction costs of doing so would be huge. A solution that would permit states to avail themselves of some self-initiated exception clause at no cost is no less problematic because states would likely fall prey to moral hazard. As they succumbed to the temptation to declare exception after exception, the free trade regime would spiral downward.

We will show that a more effective way of coping with uncertain interest group demands is to establish sanctions for noncompliance that are low enough to allow politicians to break the agreement when interest group benefits are great, but high enough to encourage states to obey the agreement most of the time and thereby prevent trade wars. This is, of course, precisely what the GATT does. We present our argument using two related formal models. The first deals with the case where two states both face the prospect of uncertain interest group demands. This model demonstrates why such states should establish a trade regime that contains sanctions that are too weak to ensure free trade. In order to explore how robust such a regime will be in the face of a changing interest group environment or a growing commitment to free trade, we employ a second, asymmetric model. We relax the assumption that both states have an incentive to depart periodically from the free trade standard and assume that only one of the two states faces such demands. The asymmetric model suggests that the high cost of sanctioning violations that would necessarily accompany a more effective regime makes the current GATT's system of weak sanctions extremely resistant to change.

4.2 Modeling Trade Treaties

In order to understand the kind of trade regime states should adopt when faced with uncertainty about interest group demands, and how this in turn helps us understand the way GATT operates, it is useful to begin by considering what the most effective free trade regime would be absent such uncertainty. We model bilateral trade between states A and B as a repeated game in which each state in each period chooses a level of protection $P \in [0, \infty)$ that influences the level of trade. The utility of state A is denoted $U_A(P^A, P^B)$, and the utility of state B is denoted $U_B(P^A, P^B)$. We do not specify the functional form of these utilities but instead adopt a series of plausible assumptions. These are detailed in Appendix 4.8.1 to this chapter and consist of some continuity and stability conditions and some plausible inequalities about preferences. These assumptions also contain conditions on the response functions $R_A(P_B)$ and $R_B(P_A)$, which denote the optimal single-period response of one state to a particular level of protection (e.g., tariff) chosen by the other state.

We will adopt the convention of representing the trade game as a Prisoner's Dilemma. While it can be argued that this pattern of incentives emerges from a variety of plausible circumstances (Staiger 1994, 27), we assume it has emerged from electoral and financial incentives provided by interest groups working to protect domestic products from foreign competition (Grossman and Helpman 1994). If there are under consideration two particular levels of tariffs $P^A < P_0^A$ and $P^B < P_0^B$, then the four outcomes represented by each side choosing P or P_0 form a payoff matrix of the Prisoner's Dilemma type. In this case, each side prefers higher tariffs regardless of the choice of the other side, but both sides prefer mutual cooperation to mutual defection. The model we use is more realistic, however, in that it allows cooperative gestures or cheating of any size.

Proposition 4.1 *The single period game with strategy spaces $[0, \infty)$ and payoffs given by utility functions U_A and U_B satisfying (A1)–(A6) has a unique Nash equilibrium at nonzero tariff rates. We call this equilibrium a noncooperative tariff structure.*

PROOF. See Appendix 4.8.2.

In a neighborhood of the noncooperative tariff structure denoted by (P_0^A, P_0^B), we can expand the utility function in an order-two Taylor series and apply the assumptions to determine the local form of the model and constraints on the coefficients. The next proposition identifies this form and constraints. This result is important because it provides a simple, but general, form for the utility function, which allows examination of the results of different treaties or different enforcement strategies.

Proposition 4.2 *In a neighborhood of the noncooperative tariff structure, any utility function satisfying (A1)–(A6) is approximately*

$$\begin{aligned}
U_A(P^A, P^B) &= a_A(P^B - P_0^B) + b_A(P^A - P_0^A)^2 \\
&\quad + c_A(P^A - P_0^A)(P^B - P_0^B) \\
&\quad + d_A(P^B - P_0^B)^2,
\end{aligned} \tag{4.1}$$

in which $a < 0$, $b < 0$, $c > 0$, and $|c/2b| < 1$. In this case, the reaction function for A is derived from equating the derivative to zero and is

$$R_A(P^B) = P_0^A - \frac{c_A}{2b_A}(P^B - P_0^B).$$

PROOF. See Appendix 4.8.3.

Note that, unlike the repeated Prisoner's Dilemma, the choices defined by the present model are continuous rather than discrete. Treaties can be set at any level below the noncooperative tariff rates. Cheating can be limited or flagrant. And punishments can range from a barely perceptible increase in tariffs that lasts for one period to a multiple of current tariffs that lasts indefinitely. These various choices interact in complex ways that present many opportunities for modeling.

The greater realism is purchased, as it usually is, at the cost of more difficult mathematics and the loss of visual concreteness provided by an extensive game depiction. However, as we shall see below, the benefits greatly outweigh the analytic costs. It turns out, for example, that much of what we in international relations think we know about the enforcement of cooperation—especially regarding the virtues of Tit-for-Tat—quickly disintegrates when we release the actors from the straitjacket of having only two symmetric choices and offer them instead the range of options that they actually have.

4.3 Treaty Maintenance under Perfect Information

4.3.1 Reversionary Strategies

Under the assumptions of our model, if tariff levels are high, both states have an opportunity to benefit by devising an agreement to lower them. Nevertheless, as in any situation where cooperation is problematic, there is an incentive to exploit the other party's trust; that is, it will always be the case that side A's optimal one-period response to side B's cooperative tariff level is to raise tariffs. Self-interest will prevent such cheating only if the consequences of the cheating are greater than the benefits. To achieve a situation where this disincentive exists, states must resort to what we call a *reversionary strategy*. This strategy prescribes that side A begin by observing the treaty, but if side B violates it, even modestly, side A should respond by abrogating the agreement for some specified period of time. During cooperative periods each side's tariff is supposed to be limited to $\bar{P}^A < P_0^A$ and $\bar{P}^B < P_0^B$, while in reversionary periods both sides raise tariffs to some noncooperative level. The most extreme reversionary strategy, often called the *grim strategy*, occurs when the response to any violation is permanent reversion (Abreu 1986).

A reversionary strategy is sufficient to enforce a treaty when each side knows that if it cheats it will suffer enough from the reversion that the net benefit will not be positive. Assuming that future utility is discounted by a factor δ, we have the following necessary condition for a punishment to be sufficient to enforce a treaty.

Proposition 4.3 *A reversionary strategy of T periods is sufficient to enforce a treaty* $(\bar{P}^A, \bar{P}^B)$ *if*

$$\frac{U_A(R_A(\bar{P}^B), \bar{P}^B) - U_A(\bar{P}^A, \bar{P}^B)}{(U_A(\bar{P}^A, \bar{P}^B) - U_A(P_0^A, P_0^B))} \leq \frac{\delta_A - \delta_A^{T+1}}{1 - \delta_A} \tag{4.2}$$

and similarly for B, where δ_A is A's discount factor for future utility.

PROOF. See Appendix 4.8.4.

Equation (4.2) implies that the longer the reversion period, the more "cooperative" the treaty (or the greater the reduction in tariffs) that can be enforced. To make this more concrete, consider an example. Suppose that A's one-period utility is given by

$$\begin{aligned} U_A(P^A, P^B) &= -(P^B - 100) - (P^A - 100)^2 \\ &\quad + .9(P^A - 100)(P^B - 100) \\ &\quad + .1(P^B - 100)^2 \end{aligned} \tag{4.3}$$

and B's by

$$\begin{aligned} U_B(P^A, P^B) &= -(P^A - 100) - (P^B - 100)^2 \\ &\quad + .9(P^B - 100)(P^A - 100) \\ &\quad + .1(P^A - 100)^2. \end{aligned} \tag{4.4}$$

Here the noncooperative treaty is at tariff levels of 100 for each side, and plausible treaties would be symmetric reductions in tariffs for each

TABLE 4.1:

Required Reversion Periods to Support Various Treaties

Treaty Tariff	One-Period Utility	Net from Cheating	$(\delta = .9)$ Periods	$(\delta = .95)$ Periods
95	5	8	2	2
90	10	30	4	4
85	15	68	7	6
80	20	121	11	8
70.25	29.75	268	∞	13
70	30	272	—	13
60	40	484	—	20
50	50	756	—	31
40	60	1089	—	61
37.19	62.81	1193	—	∞

side. Of course, in the multiperiod model, the feasibility of maintaining this treaty depends on the discount factor, δ, as well as on the previous parameters. In this case, we use two discount factors, $\delta = .9$, corresponding to an interest rate of 10 percent, and $\delta = .95$, corresponding to an interest rate of 5 percent.

Table 4.1 shows the reversion periods necessary to support treaties of various sizes (i.e., the shortest punishments consistent with satisfying condition (4.2)). A period that was any shorter would make the treaty vulnerable to cheating because it would be insufficient to remove all of the gains from violating the treaty. The table contains a number of important points. First, the temptation to cheat in this model rises rapidly with the cooperativeness of the treaty, while the treaty benefits rise less rapidly—this is what imposes a limit on which treaties can be supported. Second, this increase in the ratio of the benefit of cheating to the one-period benefit of the treaty means that increasingly severe punishments are necessary to deter defection—here severity means length of reversion—as the benefits of the treaty and corresponding restrictiveness of its requirements increase. Third, the dramatic effect of discounting the future on the viability of treaty maintenance strategies is apparent in the lesser range of feasibility and harsher punishments that are required when δ is smaller.

TABLE 4.2:

Best Treaties Supportable by Reversion with No Observational Error

Defection Period	$\delta = .9$		$\delta = .95$	
	Best Treaty	One-Period Utility	Best Treaty	One-Period Utility
∞	70.2	29.8	37.2	62.8
10	80.6	19.4	74.8	25.2
5	87.8	12.2	85.8	14.2
3	91.9	8.1	91.0	9.0
2	94.4	5.7	93.9	6.1
1	97.0	3.0	96.9	3.1

When considering these points, it is important to keep in mind something all too easily forgotten with too much exposure to two-by-two games. In determining the appropriate punishment for a treaty violation, the *only* relevant criterion is that the punishment must hurt the transgressor at least as much as the transgressor gains by the violation. This is *not* a requirement that a certain amount of trade restriction should be punished by an equal trade restriction (Tit-for-Tat). *Nor* is the criterion that the transgressor be punished at least as much as the transgressor's violation hurt the other party. Although both of these standards possess aspects of "fairness," neither is relevant to supporting the treaty equilibrium. Fairness and justice must take a back seat to the correct disincentive.

Another way to examine the relationship of treaty cooperativeness and length of punishment is to determine the best treaty that can be obtained with a given length of punishment. Table 4.2 contains the results of such determinations for the example utilities: longer punishments once again yield better results. The benefits of longer punishments rise rapidly in percentage terms as the punishment period rises above one; for example, a two-period punishment can support an equilibrium whose one-period utility (5.7) is nearly twice that of the best equilibrium supported by one-period punishment (3.0). Although the rate of increase in utility with the increase in punishment length decreases, the utility obtainable by very long punishments (29.8) is still many times that of the utility obtainable with punishment lengths of one or two periods.

Since more cooperative treaties benefit both sides more than less co-operative ones, and since (under the current model) such treaties will always be observed in equilibrium, the message of this analysis seems clear: states should always negotiate the most cooperative treaty possi-ble and enforce it by using the grim strategy. Actually, this turns out to be not quite the case because of a problem with the logic underlying the grim strategy. It is not that two grim strategies fail to form a Nash equilibrium. Under modest conditions about δ, neither side has an in-centive to change its strategy unilaterally, since mutual defection has a lower payoff than mutual treaty observance. Nor is the problem one of subgame perfection. This is simply a requirement that at any point in the game, the strategies of the two sides in the continuation of the game from that point on should be in a Nash equilibrium. This condition is to hold at *all* points, even those that might not be thought likely (or possi-ble) to occur. Consider the grim strategy. While in the treaty state, the strategies are in equilibrium, so neither side is ever expected to violate the treaty. But suppose that, for whatever reason, side A violates the treaty. Under the grim strategy, both side A and side B are expected to defect from that day forward. Given that, neither side has an incentive unilaterally to behave otherwise, and thus an equilibrium of two grim strategies is subgame perfect.

The problem lies in a third equilibrium concept mentioned briefly in chapter 2: renegotiation proofness. Although different technical defini-tions have been suggested (Abreu, Pearce, and Stacchetti 1989; Benoit and Krishna 1988; Bernheim, Peleg, and Whinston 1987; Bernheim and Ray 1990; Farrell and Maskin 1989; Pearce 1988; van Damme 1989), renegotiation proofness under any of these refers to the credibility of a threat that is harsher than that necessary to deter a particular behav-ior and costly to apply. The basic concept is well illustrated by two grim strategies. Suppose that the game, somehow, departs from the equilibrium path. The grim strategy prescribes that the actor that feels wronged should now punish the violator by abrogating the treaty and initiating a program of high tariffs that will continue forever. Regard-less of its original intent, then, the other state will follow suit because the best response to perpetual defection is perpetual defection, and loss of free trade will be permanent. Let us suppose, however, that after a significant period of time, the side that violated the treaty proposes that the two sides let bygones be bygones and return to the cooperative equilibrium. Since as of that moment such a solution is better for both parties than is continuing the trade war, they might return to some form of cooperation. Yet the likely prospect of this happening means that the original threat to defect forever was not credible—the original equilibrium was not renegotiation proof. (See Devereux (1993) and Staiger (1994) for another argument on the noncredibility of perpetual defection in trade.)

Unfortunately, there is no clear consensus about what other punishments should be ruled out on the grounds of renegotiation proofness. One can argue that a punishment of one thousand years is enough like an infinite punishment that it too should not be considered credibly renegotiation proof, but what is the absolute limit? One hundred years? Ten years? Five years? While we do not yet have a method of determining the absolute maximum punishment, we know that in any given case the defection period cannot be any longer than the period that is needed to remove any incentive to violate the treaty. If it is, it will be subject to renegotiation by the same logic that rules out the grim strategy. Just how long the period of punishment necessary to cancel out these violation benefits will be depends on the cooperativeness of the treaty, as the tables have already told us. In Table 4.2 a defection period of 10 would not be renegotiation proof in the context of a treaty that reduced tariff levels to 97.0 because it is longer than necessary. Both states would be better off if the punishment were reduced to 1. If, however, the treaty level were lowered to 80.6, that same punishment would be renegotiation proof.

We see that renegotiation proofness places a limit on the size of the threat that should be used to support any given treaty and on the absolute limit of the threat that can ever be used to enforce cooperation, but the general principle remains intact: harsher threats will support greater amounts of cooperation. This leads us to expect that institutions designed to maintain free trade will prescribe harsh penalties for violations. However, this turns out not to be the case. The GATT is notoriously vague about retaliatory sanctions. Generally, it adopts the approach that, if a state violates the agreement by establishing a tariff, negotiations should take place to insure that such increases are compensated by reductions in other areas. If these negotiations break down, abused states are entitled to do no more than withdraw "substantially equivalent concessions" (Sykes 1990, 321). This sounds suspiciously like Tit-for-Tat. Is it more effective than the analysis just completed would lead us to believe?

4.3.2 Reciprocity and Tit-for-Tat

In Tit-for-Tat, side A observes the treaty on the first turn and subsequently plays whatever level B played in the previous turn. Two Tit-for-Tats can be a Nash equilibrium, but as we will show below, there is a smaller range of treaties for which this is true than there is for the reversionary strategies. That is, reciprocity as a punishment for transgression is not as effective as larger punishments in enforcing cooperative agreements.

Strictly speaking, Tit-for-Tat facing Tit-for-Tat is not subgame perfect.[1] Tit-for-Tat *with apology* passes this test, however. In this version, both sides pursue Tit-for-Tat, except that if A somehow defects, then A cooperates on the next two trials unconditionally. B will defect one period (which punishes A's transgression) and then will also return to cooperation. This is sometimes sufficient to insure a subgame perfect equilibrium, depending on the treaty itself and on the discount rate. Specifically, if a treaty is in effect at $(\bar{P}^A, \bar{P}^B)$ and side A defects to P_t^A at time t, then A must "apologize" by playing $\bar{P}^A$ at time $t+1$ while B follows Tit-for-Tat and plays P_t^A. At time $t+2$, both return to the treaty. More generally, B plays Tit-for-Tat after a defection by A until A returns unilaterally to the treaty for one period, in which case both then return.[2]

This slightly modified Tit-for-Tat—with apology—is renegotiation proof because the punishment phase is only one period long, which is the shortest possible length and thus cannot be reduced. Unfortunately, the advantage that this modest punishment provides in insuring the strategy's renegotiation proofness has a serious drawback. The lower disincentive it provides against violations reduces the benefit level of the treaties it can support.

To see which treaties can be enforced by Tit-for-Tat, we begin with the minimal requirement that the discounted expected value to A of the treaty is greater than what A could gain by exploiting B. For example,

---

[1] If one player somehow strays from the equilibrium path and the other side defects in response, it starts a cycle of alternating defection and cooperation. In period 1, A defects and B cooperates. In period 2, A cooperates and B defects, and so forth. At this point there is no Nash equilibrium. In period 3, for example, A, who is scheduled to defect, could instead cooperate, unilaterally introducing a superior continuation.

[2] Note that this strategy has now become quite a bit more complicated than Tit-for-Tat, and there is some question as to whether it deserves the same name; certainly, any further alteration of the strategy to repair additional defects would take it out of the realm of Tit-for-Tat. We avoid the fairly common locution of calling *any* response short of the grim strategy Tit-for-Tat. Tat-for-Tat, if it means something narrower than any response, must refer to a response of equal quantity.

if a treaty at 90 is proposed (using the above illustration) and $\delta = .9$, then the value of the treaty is 10 per period, for an overall value of 100. The most exploitative possible behavior that A could adopt would be to make the unilateral best response at each turn, leading to the following path: $(95.5, 90)$, $(97.975, 95.5)$,..., which has utility to A given by

$$40.35 + .9(10.625) + .81(3.2654) + \cdots < 100.$$

Thus, a treaty at 90 is sustainable by Tit-for-Tat.

What is the limit of enforceability for Tit-for-Tat? Calculations similar to the one above show that under Tit-for-Tat A gets more utility out of adhering to the treaty than from defecting so long as the treaty amount is greater than 77.51. This compares with a treaty level of 70.25 that can be enforced by finite reversion of sufficient length.

In fact, however, there is another condition that Tit-for-Tat needs to satisfy. If the treaty is to be enforced by Tit-for-Tat with apology, then in order to obtain the good that comes of the future value of the treaty, A needs to be willing to submit to cooperating while B defects. This is not a situation that has much resonance with empirical researchers, because they rarely, if ever, see it occur. In the vast majority of cases, states that violate an agreement continue to do so while they are being punished. Let us see why.

For the illustrated utilities, if $\delta = .9$ and a treaty at 80 is contemplated, then A would benefit from the treaty compared with defection, since the treaty yields a utility of 200, while the most exploitative possible behavior yields only 182. But suppose that the defection happens anyway; that is, somehow the states depart from the equilibrium path. At that point, A's cooperative choice would cost -220.9 to take the punishment, with a future benefit to the treaty of $(.9)20/(1 - .9) = 180$, for a net utility of -40.9. By contrast, continuing the exploitation would yield 45.1. This means that A would not submit to the punishment and the treaty would unravel. In other words, Tit-for-Tat with apology at a treaty of 80 is not subgame perfect. If we require subgame perfection, the best treaty that can be enforced at $\delta = .9$ is 86.62 (compared with 70.25 for reversion) and the best treaty that can be enforced at $\delta = .95$ is 71.31 (compared with 37.19 for reversion).

Once again, the results of the analysis leave our basic conclusion intact. Even in the absence of observational errors (a well-known problem for Tit-For-Tat that we will eventually consider), reciprocity cannot support as much cooperation as reversionary strategies based on harsher, longer punishments. Were the architects of GATT blind to this logic? Is the logic incorrect? Or is something missing from our specification?

4.4 Interest Group Uncertainty

One possibility is that our emphasis on enforcement and its role in preserving free trade is simply misplaced. This would be the argument of those scholars of cooperation and international law such as Chayes and Chayes (1990a, 1990b, and 1993) and Young (1979, 1989) who believe that the high average rate of compliance with international agreements provides good evidence that compliance is not a problem, and that violations are best viewed as isolated administrative breakdowns. As Chayes and Chayes put it, "...performance that seems for some reason unsatisfactory represents a problem to be solved by mutual consultation and analysis, rather than an offense that should be punished" (1993, 5).

We find this explanation unsatisfactory. The incentive for states to violate an agreement varies enormously. The fact that enforcement plays little or no role in preventing states from violating international rules governing traffic at sea or international flight control procedures is unremarkable. They would gain virtually nothing. However, this tells us little about the role of enforcement in preventing states from violating an agreement that requires a steep reduction in tariffs. In this case, a state that could violate the agreement without being punished would stand to gain a substantial benefit. Data about the average rate of compliance might be telling us little more than that most international agreements resemble flight control agreements more than they resemble a strict tariff agreement. Since we have reason to believe that the former are easier to negotiate than the latter, and since the choice of which agreements to negotiate is endogenous, we would expect this to be the case.

This logic would lead us to expect that in the absence of strong sanctions for noncompliance there would be far more violations of GATT and the postwar free trade regime than there is of the average international agreement. This has indeed been the case. While tariffs have declined steadily in the past forty years, nontariff barriers and other discriminatory practices have proliferated. As Babai (1993, 344) notes:

> "Voluntary export restraints" (VERs) and "orderly marketing arrangements" (OMAs)—market restricting agreements that are often quotas in all but name and that are outright evasions of the MFN requirement—have become pervasive in numerous industries, in-

cluding steel, automobiles, textiles, footwear, semiconductors, electronic products, and machine tools.

The almost endless list of commonly employed discriminatory techniques includes a host of nontariff barriers in the form of health and regulatory code provisions, antidumping actions, countervailing duties, subsidies, and suspect national security claims (Jackson 1989). In recent years, for example, the United States has leveled charges of unfair practices at countries ranging from Japan to Norway, and in areas ranging from beef and corn to insurance and computer software (Bayard and Elliott 1994).

Even the North American Free Trade Act, which took effect on January 1, 1994, has already run into problems. Almost immediately the first volleys were fired of what came to be called the milk war between the United States and Mexico, as American milk began to flood Mexico. Dairymen in the state of Chihuahua responded by pushing through a 9 percent tax on milk imports, but the flow continued. By August industry lobbyists in both countries had won new protections on steel, meat, cement, and lumber; and duties on pipeline material, paper, and wheat are pending (Myerson 1994).

We believe, along with Sykes (1990) and others, that GATT's weak enforcement norm is a result of uncertainty about the future demands of interest groups.[3] States did not want aggressive enforcement of the GATT because most of them knew that they themselves would eventually find it advantageous to depart from the free trade standard. Not every industry, after all, is as constantly or predictably pressured by imports as the Japanese rice producers or the French dairy farmers. The sensitivity of a domestic sector to foreign competition varies as a function of changes in things such as labor costs, manufacturing and agricultural technology, transportation costs, and exchange rates. As these change, so do the benefits represented by a free trade standard. While it might be worth it for states to tie themselves firmly to the mast of free trade if every other state agreed to do likewise, it also might not.

In order to evaluate the logic of this argument and to understand the tradeoffs involved, we need to build a formal model that captures the incentives created by uncertain interest group demands. Let the utility of state A in normal times be as described above in (4.1) and specifically with the parameter values in (4.3) and (4.4). Periodically,

---

[3] For an explanation of GATT enforcement that focuses on the ongoing negotiation of numerous exceptions see Morrow (1993).

however, domestic pressures to apply tariffs become strong. We model this by assuming that domestic pressures are high in each period with independent probabilities p_A and p_B. When that is the case, A's utility is altered by the addition of the terms $e_A(P^A - P_0^A) + f_A$, with $e_A, f_A > 0$, and similarly for B. This additional term provides extra benefit for increased tariffs. (Values used for illustration are $p_A = p_B = 0.1$, $e_A = e_B = 2$, $f_A = f_B = 5$).

More explicitly, there are two independent sequences of Bernoulli random variables $\zeta_t^A \sim \text{Bernoulli}(p_A)$ and $\zeta_t^B \sim \text{Bernoulli}(p_B)$, and the utility functions of A and B are defined as follows:

$$
\begin{aligned}
U_A(P^A, P^B) &= a_A(P^B - P_0^B) + b_A(P^A - P_0^A)^2 \\
&\quad + c_A(P^A - P_0^A)(P^B - P_0^B) + d_A(P^B - P_0^B)^2 \\
&\quad + [e_A(P^A - P_0^A) + f_A]\zeta_t^A \qquad (4.5) \\
U_B(P^A, P^B) &= a_B(P^A - P_0^A) + b_B(P^B - P_0^B)^2 \\
&\quad + c_B(P^A - P_0^A)(P^B - P_0^B) + d_B(P^A - P_0^A)^2 \\
&\quad + [e_B(P^B - P_0^B) + f_B]\zeta_t^B. \qquad (4.6)
\end{aligned}
$$

Because the intensity of interest group pressure and an administration's ability to withstand it are difficult for even political insiders–much less voters–to estimate correctly, we will assume that ζ_t^A is unobserved by B and ζ_t^B is unobserved by A.

Now A will defect whenever the (unobservable to B) value of ζ_t^A is 1, regardless of the threatened punishment, and B will behave similarly. In periods that are mutually normal, each will abide by the treaty if the threatened sanction outweighs the advantage of defection. Discounting the expected value of the future is complicated because each side has stochastically foreseeable changes in utility that will lead to random behavioral changes, even in equilibrium.

Table 4.3 shows some numerical results using the same parameter values as the previous examples. Once again, the "best treaty" for each period is the one that yields the highest utility provided that it is enforceable; that is, it must provide a higher utility than a policy of deliberate unilateral defection. The table makes it clear that the consequences of uncertain domestic demands for protection are considerable. In this case, the optimal punishment period and associated treaty is reduced from a grim strategy—or as close as the standard of renegotiation proofness allows us to get to the grim strategy—to a defection period

TABLE 4.3:

Best Treaties When Domestic Pressures Can Occur

Defection Period	$\delta = .9$		$\delta = .95$	
	Best Treaty	Overall Utility	Best Treaty	Overall Utility
∞	95.50	13.89	94.92	20.77
10	95.96	15.94	95.67	29.43
5	96.57	17.56	96.36	34.26
4	96.81	17.89	96.63	35.32
3	**97.15**	**18.03**	**97.00**	**36.03**
2	97.66	17.57	97.54	35.48
1	98.50	14.96	98.44	30.50

NOTE: Results for the optimal period are in boldface.

of three for either value of the discount factor. While the exact result is obviously dependent on the parameter values used, the qualitative result seems robust. The existence of domestic pressures and the consequent defections limit the length of punishment that should be used and limit the cooperativeness of practical treaties to a level that provides only small improvements in the total level of unrestricted trade over the counterfactual alternative that would exist in the absence of the treaty.

It is important to understand how the incentives created by uncertainty operate here to reduce the punishment for free trade violations. This phenomenon tilts preferences toward shorter punishment periods and therefore toward less cooperative treaties. This occurs for three reasons. First, from nation A's perspective, its own domestic constituencies may at times make defection all but impossible to resist, so A will wish the consequent punishment period to be relatively short.[4] Second, B's domestic pressures will sometimes result in defection. In order to maintain the treaty, A must participate in the reversion phase, but knowing that B will likely be willing to return to cooperation when the crisis passes, A prefers that the reversion period not be too long. Finally, the defections that result from rising domestic pressure are very costly if the

---

[4]That there is a punishment period at all is a consequence of assuming that nation A's domestic pressures are not directly observable by nation B. Punishment cannot be waived simply because A asserts that there is domestic pressure, because this would induce a severe moral hazard problem.

treaty prescribes very cooperative tariff levels. This makes such high levels of cooperation too risky to be practical.[5]

All of this is not meant to imply, of course, that states would be even better off if they dispensed with penalties entirely. The reciprocity standard or some facsimile still functions to prevent the degeneration of the trade regime by providing states with a modest disincentive for responding to the demands of every protectionist interest. This reduces the number of violations that would occur to below what would take place in the absence of any penalty for defection and, by setting a standard for retaliation, it reduces the likelihood that the state that is the victim of the violation will decide to enter into a serious trade war. The compensation principle that seeks to avoid retaliation entirely by trading a rise in tariffs in one area for a negotiated decrease in another functions in the same fashion. The only difference is that, by saving the injured state the costs of retaliation, it offers greater efficiency.

4.5 Asymmetric Preferences

We have so far considered the situation where states share a common interest in being able to respond periodically to the protectionist interests within their borders. This is a reasonable representation of many, perhaps even most, situations. Yet it is also true that states are rarely equally protectionist—their commitments to the principles of free trade are sometimes radically dissimilar. One state may be convinced that it will never want to violate free trade, but it may anticipate that interest group pressure in the other state will be such that it will be forced to periodically violate any agreement. When this is the case, what sort of trade regime is likely to evolve?

Consider the situation of a state A whose utilities are described by the stable equation

$$
\begin{aligned}
U_A(P^A, P^B) \quad = \quad & -(P^B - 100) - (P^A - 100)^2 \\
& + .9(P^A - 100)(P^B - 100) \\
& + .1(P^B - 100)^2,
\end{aligned}
$$

---

[5]Another interpretation of this result concerns the strength and duration of punishment for transgressions. The uncertainty caused by domestic pressure means that punishments that are employed should be of shorter duration and lesser magnitude, since they will have to be imposed even in equilibrium. The punishment is smaller in magnitude in the case where domestic pressures exist because the treaty calls for smaller cuts in tariffs; reversion is therefore a smaller sanction.

TABLE 4.4:
Best Treaties under Asymmetric Domestic Pressure

Defection Period	$\delta = .9$		$\delta = .95$	
	Best Treaty	Overall Utility	Best Treaty	Overall Utility
∞	95.50	10.66	95.50	13.97
10	95.64	12.75	95.50	22.98
5	96.34	14.28	96.10	27.82
4	**96.62**	**14.50**	96.41	28.71
3	97.01	14.46	**98.84**	**29.05**
2	97.56	13.66	97.44	27.81
1	98.44	10.66	98.37	21.90

NOTE: Results for the optimal period are in boldface.

with B alone subject to domestic pressures and having utility function

$$
\begin{aligned}
U_B(P^A, P^B) \;=\; & -(P^A - P_0^A) - (P^B - P_0^B)^2 \\
& + .9(P^A - P_0^A)(P^B - P_0^B) + .1(P^A - P_0^A)^2 \\
& + [2(P^B - P_0^B) + 5]\zeta_t^B.
\end{aligned}
$$

A no longer needs to reserve the right to defect when domestic pressures dictate, because from A's point of view, an important reason for limiting the level of punishment has disappeared. Yet A knows that this can happen to B, although it is never sure when the pressures are sufficiently intense to force a defection. Table 4.4 shows the result of this one-sided domestic pressure on the optimal treaty. A comparison with Table 4.3 reveals that the effect produced by the possibility of the other side defecting due to domestic pressure is surprisingly similar to the result when both sides suffer such pressure. In particular, a short reversion period is optimal for A, even when A has no domestic pressure but B does.

Of course, these results reflect the fact that the strength of B's domestic constituencies is assumed to be so great that the government invariably capitulates to their demands. Because of this, A has no threats available that are intimidating enough to prevent B from defecting in those periods when domestic considerations arise. Clearly, this need not be the case. Whether it is the case or not depends on the size of the parameter e_B, which models the additional utility B gains from higher protectionism in those periods in which domestic constituencies are active.[6]

Were we wrong to assume that the demands of B's constituencies were so irresistible? Can A reasonably believe that it can eliminate B's propensity to capitulate to interest groups by increasing the severity of the (renegotiation proof) punishment for defection? Without an elaborate empirical study it is difficult to know. However, casual observation provides a hint. Clearly, if B's domestic interests are very weak (e_B is small), only a modest increase in punishment is needed from the level needed to enforce the agreement in the absence of domestic pressure. If B's domestic interests are very strong, no punishment would be sufficient. For intermediate values of e_B, a large increase in punishment would be necessary. In the first of these cases, we would observe modest punishments deterring defection. In the third, we would observe large punishments deterring defection. In the second case, we would see modest punishments that do not completely deter defection but that allow defection when domestic pressures are high. Only the second case appears to occur in practice. Trade sanctions rarely exceed the compensation standard by a large amount, and defection due to domestic pressures is common. This suggests that the parameter values we have used are, in fact, in the correct range.

This analysis suggests that a state which has embraced free trade and does not anticipate the need to bow to domestic pressures should not rush to increase the sanctions for trade violations. The result may be less to deter the non–free trade states than merely to increase the costs of enforcement without any consequent benefit of greater cooperation.

4.6 Coping with Nontariff Barriers: U.S. Section 301

As long as states acted in a fashion that was consistent with the compensation system or were punished with a reciprocal loss of benefits if they did not, the GATT struggled along with an "acceptable" level of violations. Although it provided a level of free trade that was less than the ideal, it compensated for this in the eyes of most states by providing the flexibility to respond to periodic demands at home. It was not long,

---

[6]We use a parameter size of $e_B = 2$ for illustration. This turns out to be just over twice the quantity ($e_B = .935$) that makes defection more attractive than cooperation in periods when domestic constituencies are active.

however, before states began succumbing to the allure of a mechanism that offered all of the flexibility of both the periodic tariff renegotiation of GATT Article XXVIII and the escape clause of Article XIX, but none of the costs. This mechanism was the nontariff barrier (NTB).

GATT's national treatment obligation, which forbids states from treating foreign products differently from domestic goods, proved of little help in coping with NTBs. States found it all too easy to create standards that applied to all goods yet created effective barriers against imports. The Tokyo round attempted to redress some of these problems by creating a new Agreement on Technical Barriers to Trade that said, in part: "Parties shall ensure that technical regulations and standards are not prepared, adopted, or applied with a view to creating obstacles to international trade" (Jackson 1990, 198). This standard was widely hailed as an improvement, but it did not end the problems with nontariff barriers.

As complaints in the United States about practices in Japan continued to mount, Congress acted to increase the ability of the U.S. to act unilaterally in retaliation for the damage done to its domestic commercial interests by the action of foreign governments. These actions culminated in the Super 301 amendments in the 1988 Omnibus Trade and Competitiveness Act, which attempted to reduce presidential discretion about whether to take action; it sought instead to make retaliation almost mandatory upon a finding of discrimination on the part of the U.S. Trade Representative (Jackson 1990b). The magnitude of the sanction reflected the earlier GATT standard. It was to be "devised so as to affect goods or services of the foreign country in an amount that is equivalent in value to the burden or restriction being imposed by that country on United States commerce" (Sykes 1990, 317).

As Sykes points out, the Section 301 standard is strikingly similar to the GATT standard. It sought to reestablish a system in which states have the option of defecting in response to irregularly occurring domestic pressures if they are willing to pay a modest price. Seen in this light, the contribution of Section 301 is that it closes the loophole of the nontariff barrier, which allowed states to defect for free.

Yet NTBs also presented another challenge. The GATT was designed to cope with tariffs that were perfectly observed by all parties. The steady shift from tariffs to nontariff measures quickly created a situation of uncertainty about the magnitude and origin of protectionist measures. Thus, trade officials representing the interests of exporters might encounter a government procurement standard, customs law, public health requirement, or safety standard but not know the extent to which it reflected either a purely domestic policy goal or an effort to stop or slow the importation of foreign goods. The difficulty was complicated further by the existence of a host of business customs and practices that are not set down in any legal code but nevertheless function to limit imports or the extent of price competition.

Section 301 provided a useful tool to cope with the general threat of nontariff barriers, but it did not in itself solve the problem of distinguishing between a nontariff barrier and a distinctive cultural practice, or a legitimate side effect of administrative law. As a practical matter, in an environment of imperfect information, someone still had to decide when to apply Section 301 and when not. This is where the use of trigger strategies comes in.

In order to explore the enforcement implications of uncertainty about either the extent to which a domestic law represents a NTB or the extent to which the state should be held responsible for the existence of an import-reducing business practice, let us return to the model without domestic pressures. Suppose that a treaty at $(\bar{P}^A, \bar{P}^B)$ is agreed upon but that A observes, not B's actual trade restriction P_t^B, but a version perturbed by error, $\tilde{P}_t^B = P_t^B + \epsilon_t^B$, and vice versa for B's observation of A's trade restriction. Assume that ϵ^A and ϵ^B are independent normal with mean zero and variance σ_ϵ^2. Even if B exactly observes the treaty, A's estimate of B's production will be above the treaty amount half the time. Hence, the probability of reversion due to this estimate of B's production will be .5 under any of the punishment strategies examined so far. Since the probability of reversion due to A is also independently .5, the chance of the treaty continuing is only .25, and the expected length of the treaty will be only $1/.75 = 1.3$ periods. It follows that the same problem applies to Tit-for-Tat, with or without apology. Hence, none of these strategies will generate much cooperation.

Clearly, we have to find a way to reduce the sensitivity of our compliance strategy to allow for the observational error, but this needs to be done in a way that leaves no incentive for cheating under the guise of noise. Trigger strategies constitute a class of strategies that can be used for this purpose. (See the discussion in Chapter 2; and Green and Porter 1984; Porter 1983; Downs and Rocke 1990.) The basic idea is simple. Side A introduces a trigger level Π_A that takes the expected level of observational error into consideration. If B's observed trade restriction level $\tilde{P}_t^B$ exceeds Π_A, then A, as a punishment, reverts to a trade war for periods $t+1, t+2, \ldots, t+T_A$. If A reverts, so does B. Side B introduces its own trigger level and duration. Together, these strategies will be in equilibrium and will enforce the treaty if neither side has an incentive to produce more than the treaty amount during cooperative periods.[7]

If we add to the definition of the strategy that each side chooses the optimal tariff amount given the triggers, we obtain a complete specification, as follows: First, define the conditions for cooperation and reversion and transitions between them.

1. There are two states of the world, cooperation ($C_t = 1$) and reversion ($C_t = 0$), with $C_0 = 1$.
2. If $C_t = 1$ and $P_t^A \leq \Pi_B$ and $P_t^B \leq \Pi_A$, then $C_{t+1} = 1$.
3. If $C_t = 1$ and either $P_t^A > \Pi_B$ or $P_t^B > \Pi_A$, then $C_{t+1} = 0$.
4. Let $t^* = \min_\tau \{\tau | C_{t-\tau} = 1\}$ and $T = \max(T_A, T_B)$. If $C_t = 0$ and $t^* < T$, then $C_{t+1} = 0$.
5. If $C_t = 0$ and $t^* = T$, then $C_{t+1} = 1$.

Next define the trade restriction choices for A and B.

1. If $C_t = 1$, then $P_t^A = \bar{P}^A$ and $P_t^B = \bar{P}^B$.
2. If $C_t = 0$, then $P_t^A = P_0^A$ and $P_t^B = P_0^B$.[8]

It can be shown that an equilibrium exists for every choice of sufficiently large enforcement periods T_A and T_B (see Downs and Rocke 1990). While it may not seem obvious, the trigger levels and reversion periods cannot be unilaterally changed by one of the players, since the strategies of both players call for reversion whenever either exceeds the announced trigger.

There are two conditions that must hold for each of A and B in order for a trigger strategy equilibrium to exist.

---

[7]For the time being, we are assuming that the *intensity* of the punishment is fixed and that only the duration varies. Reversion to a trade war as a specific punishment has several advantages. It reduces the complexity of the analysis by eliminating one decision-variable. It fixes that variable at a point where neither side has a short-term incentive to depart from the punishment regime; this means that the punishment condition is stable until mutual consent returns the condition to the treaty.

[8]This is, of course, a highly simplified model. Strictly speaking, actual GATT and Section 301 punishments do not involve large departures from the treaty, although it is not clear whether this is because the agreements do not call for tariff reductions that are greatly below the Nash level, or because punishment does not involve defection to the Nash level. In fact, it is hard to say in any real case what the Nash equilibrium to which reversion would be. Even more complications are introduced by the fact that GATT and Section 301 compensation and punishment are often in another trade area from that of a violation, so that a complete model would be multivariate. We avoid these complexities and stick to our simplified model, because we believe that it captures some essential truths about the process. Nor are we convinced that the extra elaboration of a multivariate model would yield insight proportional to the effort.

For the first, which turns out in general to be more restrictive, A must prefer the treaty to behaving exploitatively. If A could profit by playing the best response to B's treaty amount, reverting for T periods, and then immediately defecting again, then the treaty could never be upheld. This is qualitatively the same behavior that needed to be deterred in earlier examples. For the second, small changes in A's trade restriction choice must produce no net profit or loss; that is, A needs to be deterred from chipping away at the margins under the cover of noise. This means that the derivative of the value function of the equilibrium with respect to A's production must be zero.

We do not give a complete proof here, since it parallels that in Downs and Rocke (1990), but a few details may be enlightening. First, the value V_A of a treaty satisfies the recursion

$$
\begin{aligned}
V_A &= U_A(\bar{P}^A, \bar{P}^B) + (1 - p_A)(1 - p_B)\delta_A V_A \\
&\quad + (1 - (1 - p_A)(1 - p_B)) \left[\frac{\delta_A - \delta_A^{T+1}}{1 - \delta_A} U_A(P_0^A, P_0^B) \right. \\
&\quad \left. + \delta_A^{T+1} V_A \right]
\end{aligned}
$$

so that

$$
V_A = \frac{U_A(\bar{P}^A, \bar{P}^B) + (1 - (1 - p_A)(1 - p_B))\frac{\delta_A - \delta_A^{T+1}}{1 - \delta_A} U_A(P_0^A, P_0^B)}{1 - (1 - p_A)(1 - p_B)\delta_A - (1 - (1 - p_A)(1 - p_B))\delta_A^{T+1}},
$$

where

$$
p_A = \Pr(\tilde{P}_t^A > \Pi_B) = \Pr(P_t^A + \epsilon_t > \Pi_B) = 1 - \mathrm{F}(\Pi_B - P_t^A),
$$

and where F is the distribution function of ϵ, the observational error (p_B is defined similarly). We can let $U_A(P_0^A, P_0^B) = 0$, without loss of generality, so this expression reduces to

$$
V_A = \frac{U_A(\bar{P}^A, \bar{P}^B)}{1 - (1 - p_A)(1 - p_B)\delta_A - (1 - (1 - p_A)(1 - p_B))\delta_A^{T+1}}. \tag{4.7}
$$

We can determine if A is deterred from cheating at the margins by checking if $\partial V_A / \partial \bar{P}^A = 0$. This is sufficient, since if any one period's tariff could be profitably changed, then so could all of them, because of the renewal nature of the process of reversion and cooperation. One can easily check that the condition is

$$
\begin{aligned}
\frac{\partial V_A}{\partial \bar{P}^A} &= \frac{\frac{\partial U_A(\bar{P}^A, \bar{P}^b)}{\partial \bar{P}^A} D - U_A(\bar{P}^A, \bar{P}^B)\frac{\partial p_A}{\partial \bar{P}^A}(1 - p_B)(\delta - \delta^{T+1})}{D^2} \\
&= 0,
\end{aligned}
$$

TABLE 4.5:

Best Treaties Supportable by Trigger Strategies in the Presence of Observational Error: $\delta = .9$

Defection Period	Best Treaty		One-Period Utility	
	GATT	301	GATT	301
∞	70.3	75.8	29.8	24.2
10	80.6	84.8	19.4	15.2
5	87.8	91.0	12.2	9.0
3	91.9	94.6	8.1	4.4
2	94.4	96.9	5.7	3.1
1	97.0	—	3.0	—

where D is the denominator of (4.7). For the example utility function, this can be solved for every treaty and for every reversion period of length greater than one period.

We can obtain a qualitative idea of the cost of the uncertainty induced by NTBs by comparing a GATT-type punishment for perfectly observed defections, as analyzed in Section 4.3.1, with a 301-type trigger punishment, as described in this section. For expositional purposes, and in order to compare like quantities, we describe the results for the simplified version in which punishment consists of reversion to the Nash level. Tables 4.5 and 4.6 compare these two for two levels of the discount factor δ. The treaties under 301 are all less cooperative than those under GATT, and the utility generated is less, often by a factor of nearly two. For example, when $\delta = .9$ and a two-period punishment is to be used, a GATT-type treaty with no observational error can achieve a one-period utility of 5.7. The introduction of nontariff barriers, and the consequent appearance of observational error requiring a trigger strategy, lowers the utility to 3.1.

The use of NTBs rather than tariffs has important negative consequences for the ability of treaties to produce freer trade, and it works to everyone's disadvantage (even the state using them). The reasons are complex. First, the uncertainty created by NTBs will cause the imposition of punishments on states that are not violating the agreement. This happens because the trigger in a trigger strategy needs to be close

TABLE 4.6:

Best Treaties Supportable by Trigger Strategies in the Presence of Observational Error: $\delta = .95$

Defection Period	Best Treaty		One-Period Utility	
	GATT	301	GATT	301
∞	37.2	47.2	62.8	52.8
10	74.8	79.8	25.2	20.3
5	85.8	89.2	14.2	10.8
3	91.0	93.8	9.0	6.2
2	93.9	96.4	6.1	3.6
1	96.9	—	3.1	—

enough to the agreed-upon level such that a small increase in protectionism would produce an increase in the probability of reversions sufficient to outweigh the gains of cheating. This in turn requires that the trigger be near enough to the treaty level that accidental defection can occur. Thus, the uncertainty generated by NTBs can create the appearance of a violation even when both sides are, in fact, adhering to the agreement. Second, the regimes that can be supported in the presence of this uncertainty are less cooperative than those that could be accommodated under the easy observation of tariffs. This means that even during nonreversionary periods, all obtain less benefit under NTBs than they would under the more cooperative regimes possible with tariffs. Finally, the lesser benefit of the treaty changes the balance between the temptation to defect and the treaty benefits. As a result, defection becomes more likely, and the agreement is harder to support.

4.7 Conclusion

The structure of the international trade regime provides a striking example of how domestic uncertainty shapes the operation of international institutions. The analysis suggests that it is uncertainty about the payoffs associated with the demands of interest groups, rather than the demands themselves or some system-level characteristic, that determines how states will be penalized for violating the free trade norms of the system. Penalties that would clearly be suboptimal in a world where state utility is determined solely by gains from trade and lower consumer prices are shown to offer real advantages when politicians are also concerned with campaign contributions and electoral success.

With its compensation principle that promises Pareto-efficient defections and backup remedy of withdrawal of concessions, the GATT discourages protectionist measures but does not harshly sanction them. The modest sanction is enough to keep states from abusing a costless escape clause and helps coordinate the expectations of states in such a way that a trade war of spiraling retaliations and counterretaliations is avoided.

Although the underlying logic of the system is clearest in a trading world made up of democratic governments that do not know how much free trade they want to commit themselves to, not every state has to face protectionist domestic interests for the equilibrium to hold. According to our simulations, even if a state is certain that it will always prefer a system in which there are no barriers to trade, it should usually avoid the temptation to punish its unreliable partners at the harsh level that would be optimal to preserve a true free trade norm. Domestic interests in those states would still be likely to push through their protectionist agenda and any change would be for the worse. The liberal state would lose the cost of the sanction as well as the benefit of the free trade.

Although the original GATT solution represented a successful balance between the expected welfare benefits provided by free trade and the expected agency benefits provided by the ability to respond flexibly to interest group demands, it proved to be unstable. States quickly discovered that they could avoid both GATT's compensatory standard and the retaliatory withdrawal of benefits by using a wide variety of nontariff barriers that either were not explicitly proscribed by the GATT or were difficult to eradicate by standard GATT procedures. In response the United States created and then refined Section 301 guidelines to permit unilateral retaliation for this new variety of protection, much as federal law might be extended to cope with a new type of securities law violation.

Significantly, the character of the sanctions outlined in Section 301 demonstrates the same respect for the exigencies of interest group uncertainty as does the GATT itself. Just as the theory predicts, the standard for retaliation in this new arena is substantially less than the level needed to offset the benefits of protection and to keep protectionist efforts from recurring. The mechanism of protection may have changed but the influence of uncertainty in domestic politics had not.

4.8 Appendixes

4.8.1 Assumptions

(A1) U_A and U_B have two continuous partial derivatives.

(A2) It is never in A's interest for B to have a greater amount of protection; that is

$$\frac{\partial U_A(P^A, P^B)}{\partial P^B} < 0, \quad \forall P^B.$$

Similarly,

$$\frac{\partial U_B(P^A, P^B)}{\partial P^A} < 0, \quad \forall P^A.$$

(A3) For any fixed value of P^B, $U_A(P^A, P^B)$ is strictly increasing on $[0, R_A(P^B)]$ and strictly decreasing on $[R_A(P^B), \infty)$ as a function of P^A, where the position of the maximum may depend on P^B. Declining marginal returns to protectionist measures, together with linear costs are sufficient to insure this. Note that this implies that there is a unique best response $R_A(P^B)$ by A to any choice by B. Similarly, for any fixed value of P^A, $U_B(P^A, P^B)$ is strictly increasing on $[0, R_B(P^A)]$ and strictly decreasing on $[R_B(P^A), \infty)$ as a function of P^B.

(A4) $\exists \, 0 < k < 1$ such that $R'_A(P^B) \leq k$, $\forall P^B$. This is a stability condition which guarantees that there will be no trade wars with unbounded increases in tariffs. Similarly, $R'_B(P^A) \leq k \; \forall P^A$.

(A5) $R''_A(P^A) \leq 0$, $\forall P^A$ and $R''_B(P^A) \leq 0$, $\forall P^A$. These represent nonincreasing marginal returns to increases in trade protection.

(A6) $R_A(0) > 0$ and $R_B(0) > 0$. If the opponent has no tariffs or nontariff barriers, then some nonzero amount of protection is the best choice.

4.8.2 Proof of Proposition 4.1

A Nash equilibrium is a point (P_0^A, P_0^B) satisfying $R_A(P_0^B) = P_0^A$ and $R_B(P_0^A) = P_0^B$. Consider the graphs of $y = R_B(x)$ and $x = R_A(y)$. The first curve lies below $y = R_B(0) + kx$ by (A4) and the second lies above $y = k^{-1}(x - R_A(0))$ by (A4). The two bounding lines intersect at $x_0 = (R_A(0) + kR_B(0))/(1 - k^2)$ and $y_0 = (R_B(0) + kR_A(0))/(1 - k^2)$, which are positive since $k < 1$. Thus there is a Nash equilibrium $P_0^A \leq x_0$ and $P_0^B \leq y_0$. At the crossing point, the first curve is either concave down or decreasing by (A5). The second curve is either concave up or moving back to the left. Thus the first line lies below its tangent at the intersection point and the second curve lies above its tangent. Consequently, they cannot intersect again. $\square$

4.8.3   Proof of Proposition 4.2

In a neighborhood of the Nash equilibrium, a Taylor series expansion yields

$$
\begin{aligned}
U_A(P^A, P^B) \;\approx\; & U_A(P_0^A, P_0^B) + (P^A - P_0^A)\frac{\partial U_A(P^A, P^B)}{\partial P^A}\Big|_{(P_0^A, P_0^B)} \\
& + (P^B - P_0^B)\frac{\partial U_A(P^A, P^B)}{\partial P^B}\Big|_{(P_0^A, P_0^B)} \qquad (4.8) \\
& + \frac{1}{2}(P^A - P_0^A)^2\frac{\partial^2 U_A(P^A, P^B)}{\partial (P^A)^2}\Big|_{(P_0^A, P_0^B)} \\
& + (P^A - P_0^A)(P^B - P_0^B)\frac{\partial^2 U_A(P^A, P^B)}{\partial P^A \partial P^B}\Big|_{(P_0^A, P_0^B)} \\
& + \frac{1}{2}(P^B - P_0^B)^2\frac{\partial^2 U_A(P^A, P^B)}{\partial (P^B)^2}\Big|_{(P_0^A, P_0^B)} \\
=\; & U_A(P_0^A, P_0^B) + (P^B - P_0^B)\frac{\partial U_A(P^A, P^B)}{\partial P^B}\Big|_{(P_0^A, P_0^B)} \\
& + \frac{1}{2}(P^A - P_0^A)^2\frac{\partial^2 U_A(P^A, P^B)}{\partial (P^A)^2}\Big|_{(P_0^A, P_0^B)} \\
& + (P^A - P_0^A)(P^B - P_0^B)\frac{\partial^2 U_A(P^A, P^B)}{\partial P^A \partial P^B}\Big|_{(P_0^A, P_0^B)} \\
& + \frac{1}{2}(P^B - P_0^B)^2\frac{\partial^2 U_A(P^A, P^B)}{\partial (P^B)^2}\Big|_{(P_0^A, P_0^B)}. \qquad (4.9)
\end{aligned}
$$

The nature of trade competition, as exemplified by the assumptions (A1)–(A6) force some of these partial derivatives to be zero, and determine the sign of others.

1. Since (P_0^A, P_0^B) is an equilibrium, we must have

$$
\frac{\partial U_A(P^A, P^B)}{\partial P^A}\Big|_{(P_0^A, P_0^B)} = 0.
$$

2. Since A would generally prefer B to reduce the amount of protection (A2), we have

$$
\frac{\partial U_A(P^A, P^B)}{\partial P^B}\Big|_{(P_0^A, P_0^B)} < 0.
$$

3. Since the equilibrium must be a maximum of A's utility with respect to A's choice,

$$
\frac{\partial^2 U_A(P^A, P^B)}{\partial (P^A)^2}\Big|_{(P_0^A, P_0^B)} < 0.
$$

This formulation leads to a specific functional form that is valid in a neighborhood of the Nash equilibrium for any specification of utility functions that satisfies (A1)–(A6) and that is a useful illustration taken as a global definition. Suppose that

$$
\begin{aligned}
U_A(P^A, P^B) &= a_A(P^B - P_0^B) + b_A(P^A - P_0^A)^2 \\
&\quad + c_A(P^A - P_0^A)(P^B - P_0^B) \\
&\quad + d_A(P^B - P_0^B),^2
\end{aligned}
$$

and similarly for B's utility. In this case, the reaction function for A is derived from equating the derivative to zero and is

$$
R_A(P^B) = P_0^A - \frac{c_A}{2b_A}(P^B - P_0^B).
$$

Then this satisfies all the conditions if the following conditions hold ((A1) is satisfied automatically since U is a quadratic):

1. For (A2) to be true at the equilibrium, we need $a < 0$.

2. For (A3) to be true, we need $b < 0$.

3. If A is to react to an increase with an increase and to a decrease with a decrease, we need $c > 0$.

4. For (A4) to be true, we need $|c/2b| < 1$. This is a stability requirement. When this is the case, unbridled competition returns to an equilibrium level after a series of turns; if not, then any out-of-equilibrium situation would result in unbounded increases in protectionist measures.

5. (A5) is true always since the second partials of the reaction function are zero.

6. For (A6) to be true, we need

$$
P_0^A + \frac{c}{2b}P_0^B > 0
$$

which is satisfied if $P_0^A > kP_0^B$ and $P_0^B > kP_0^A$, so that the equilibrium is not too far from even. Very uneven equilibria can occur with the general model, but the global quadratic model is then no longer suitable. $\quad\square$

4.8.4   Proof of Proposition 4.3

The most A can gain from cheating if B is playing a reversionary strategy for T periods is by playing $R_A(\bar{P}^B)$ on one move, which engenders a benefit of $U_A(R_A(\bar{P}^B), \bar{P}^B) - U_A(\bar{P}^A, \bar{P}^B)$ over observing the treaty for that one period. For T subsequent periods, A incurs a cost of $U_A(\bar{P}^A, \bar{P}^B) - U_A(P_0^A, P_0^B)$, which when discounted to the present is multiplied by $(\delta_A - \delta_A^{T+1})/(1 - \delta_A)$. This whole cycle repeats at intervals of $T + 1$, so the overall utility is divided by δ_A^{T+1}. This yields the required formula. $\square$

Chapter 5
Willing but Maybe Not Able: The Impact of Uncertainty about State Capacity

Trust none;
For oaths are straws, men's faiths are wafer-cakes,
And hold-fast is the only dog, my duck.
  —Shakespeare

5.1 Introduction

In July 1994 the *Economist* published a short piece under the headline "Smelt a Rat." Representatives of the world's aluminum smelters and their governments had met in Australia to review the operation of their recent agreement to limit production and drive up prices. Notwithstanding the fact that the price of aluminum had recently skyrocketed, there was dissension in the ranks. It was widely suspected that while Western states and their producers had strictly complied with the terms of the agreement, the Russians had not reduced production capacity by the mandated 500,000 tons, and may have eliminated only 40 percent of that amount. Russia's failure to comply was attributed to the fact that the government representatives who negotiated the agreement had little control over the behavior of Russian smelters (July 1994, 64).

Stories like this are not unusual. State capacity almost always plays a pivotal role in determining the success or failure of international institutions. As Keohane, Haas, and Levy note in connection with the effectiveness of environmental institutions, "States must possess the political and administrative capacity to make the domestic adjustments necessary for the implementation of international norms, principles, or rules" (1993, 20). Unfortunately, the capacity of a state to implement

the rules connected with a particular international regulatory institution
is often difficult to estimate precisely. While almost any political scientist could have predicted that Russian negotiators in the post-Soviet era
would have more difficulty than their Western counterparts in getting
their industries to resist the temptation to overproduce, few would have
wanted to venture a guess about how much overproduction there would
be, and none would have wanted to bet very much on the accuracy of
her estimate. The same is true about state capacity estimates relating
to Chinese enforcement of the new GATT's intellectual property provisions, Ukraine's destruction of its nuclear weapons, or Eastern Europe's
reduction of pollution.

What makes estimating state capacity particularly problematic is
that it is not constant over time. It varies as a function of a variety of
factors such as the condition of a state's economy and the stability of
its political regime.[1] To appreciate this one need look no further than
the case of the aluminum cartel. No one believes that the ability of
the Russian negotiators to enforce their agreement is independent of the
state of the Russian economy, the stability of the current government, or
progress in rebuilding the Russian administrative state. Who can offer
a system of structural equations that can reliably predict the Russian
compliance rate with the aluminum cartel two years from now, let alone
five?

Our concern in this chapter is to understand how the knowledge that
state capacity is uncertain at any given time and that it also may change
in the future affects the creation and survival of multilateral international institutions. We begin by constructing a model of a multilateral
environmental agreement designed to control pollution in a body of water bordered by three states. We then introduce three uncertainties: (1)
about the exact amount of pollution being generated by any given state
(analogous to uncertainty about a particular state's aluminum production); (2) about the capacity of a state to regulate its producers; and
(3) about how a state's regulatory capacity will change over time.[2]

Our analysis reveals how these three uncertainties affect the operation and ultimately the very existence of international regulatory institutions. Even relatively modest doubts about the present capacity of a

---

[1]Obviously, the extent to which this is true varies across states. Capacity uncertainty is usually—although certainly not always—greater in developing states than
in developed states.

[2]The literature on the implications of state capacity for environmental regulation
is growing rapidly. See, for example, "Hard Road to Nuclear Waste Disposal" (1991);
Andressen (1993); Bernauer (1994); and Roginko (1994).

state to implement institutional norms can combine with equally modest expectations of capacity change to prevent states from creating a regulatory institution or lead them to terminating an existing one. These decisions are not necessarily prompted by the classic fear of exploitation. Indeed, the incentives are such that two states might well agree to continue to abide by the regulatory rules of a three-party institution they have just terminated, withdrawn from, or failed to establish. In this case, the inspiration for the demise of the larger institution flows from expectations about the cost of enforcement. The two states do not want to risk being part of an institution where the incapacity of the third leads to a large number of violations that have to be punished. The cost of increased pollution associated with unpunished violations is simply less than the combination of a slightly lower level of pollution and a much higher cost of sanctioning violations.

We argue that this dynamic has a powerful effect on the distribution of institutions in the international system. When there is a high level of uncertainty about a given state's capacity, other states will tend to include it in coordination regimes and cooperative institutions from which there is little temptation to defect, but they will systematically exclude it from institutions that are "deeply" cooperative, in the sense of requiring states to give up the substantial benefits that would stem from (unpunished) defection.[3] The anticipated costs of punishing such states for noncompliance are simply too high. This situation also suggests that determining whether it is better to approach a given environmental problem by organizing a large number of states in a relatively weak institution or by organizing a smaller number in a more demanding institution depends to a large extent on uncertainty about state capacity.

5.2   An Environmental Model

Two states that border a common body of water are considering creating an institution to manage a growing pollution problem. They must decide whether to include in that institution a third, less-developed state, with

---

[3]One way to estimate the depth of cooperation is to calculate how much it would cost various states to abide by the treaty's restrictions but gain nothing in return. For example, a treaty that required a state to reduce its emissions 30 percent as opposed to a 10 percent reduction would "cost" an uncompensated state the difference in decreased competitiveness and increased regulatory effort. Alternatively, one could estimate a treaty's level of cooperation by measuring the benefit each state would acquire by an unpunished defection from the treaty equilibrium to its previous noncooperative Nash.

a relatively unstable political regime eager to acquire the prestige of being accepted as an equal in the international community. The extent to which each country suffers from the pollution depends on the total amount of pollution generated by all three states. For each, reducing its own emissions will require an effort to regulate its industries that also imposes a cost. Since the cost of emissions reduction by each state is borne by it alone, while the benefits accrue to all the bordering nations, one has a public goods problem of the type that can generate Pareto-suboptimal solutions.

For the sake of generality, let us consider a group of n states denoted $A, B, \ldots$, with a generic state being L. For state L the level of regulation determines the annual pollution x^L emitted by that state, with the total pollution received by the sea being $X = \sum_L x^L$. The cost of pollution is related to X by a cost function $P_L(X)$ which is increasing in X. We also assume that $P_L'(X)$ exists and is increasing in X, since pollution causes harm that generally increases more than linearly with the level. For the sake of specificity in our examples, we will take this to be a quadratic function

$$P_L(X) = \alpha^L X^2.$$

The parameter α^L codes state L's vulnerability to marine pollution, which involves the length of seacoast, the fraction of the population on the coast, the amount of tourism, the type of coastal land (sandy beaches versus coastal wetlands), and so forth.

The regulatory cost that state L accepts in order to reduce its pollution from the amount M^L, which would be emitted in the absence of regulations, to a lower amount x^L is denoted $c_L(x^L)$. We assume that $c(x^L)$ is decreasing in x^L on $[0, M^L]$ and is zero for $x^L \geq M^L$, since no cost is incurred if no restriction is imposed. For the same reason, we assume the $c'(M^L) = 0$. Furthermore, $c(x^L)$ should rise arbitrarily high as $x^L \to 0$, since a zero level of pollution generation is incompatible with human occupation. One function that fits these requirements and that we use for illustration is

$$c^L = \beta^L \left[(x^L - M^L) - M^L \log(x^L/M^L) \right]. \tag{5.1}$$

Because it represents the cost of imposing a regulatory regime, the parameter β^L can be thought of as the capacity of state L to enforce an environmental regulation. While the cost function (5.1) arguably contains factors in addition to the political and administrative capacity to implement the norms of any agreement, one expects it to be directly related to that capacity.

Figure 5.1 shows these two functions, as well as the total cost

$$C_L(X) = \alpha^L X^2 + \beta^L \left[(x^L - M^L) - M^L \log(x^L/M^L) \right],$$

for parameter values $\alpha^L = 0.25$, $\beta^L = 1$, $M_L = 1$, with three states involved. In this case, we are plotting the cost to one party of its individual regulation decision, with other two parties holding firm at an established level, here taken to be 0.45. Note that the individually optimal one-period decision is one where

$$
\begin{aligned}
0 &= \frac{\partial C^L}{\partial x^L} \\
  &= 2\alpha^L X + \beta^L (1 - M^L/x_L)
\end{aligned}
$$

the positive solution to which is

$$x^L_{\text{Opt}} = \frac{-(2\alpha^L \tilde{X}^L + \beta^L) + \sqrt{(2\alpha^L \tilde{X}^L + \beta^L)^2 + 8\alpha^L \beta^L M_L}}{4\alpha^L},$$

where $\tilde{X}^L = X - x^L$ is the amount of pollution emitted by states other than L. For the parameter values used in the plot, the optimal value is 0.5755.

Now if each side adjusts its amount of regulation to the optimal value conditional on the others, the unique one-period Nash equilibrium results. In fact, the triple $(.5486, .5486, .5486)$ is the one-period Nash equilibrium in which each state chooses its individually optimal act. Note that each state is reducing its own pollution by 45 percent from the level that would exist in the absence of any government regulation. This reduction is not a by-product of the states observing each other, but rather is a result of each state reducing the pollution of its own industry to a level such that the harm it causes itself is just balanced by the regulatory cost. This is equivalent to the United States regulating sulfur emissions to a level based on acid rain within the U.S., independent of any effect it might have on Canada. The total cost of this solution to each nation is .8261.

To reduce this amount further, some form of cooperation between states is necessary. If a binding agreement could be established to set a level of regulation and thus the level of pollution emitted by each nation, then the best choice would be $(0.3732, 0.3732, 0.3732)$ (pollution is reduced by 63 percent), which imposes a total cost of .6722. This reduces the cost by almost 20 percent over the noncooperative equilibrium.

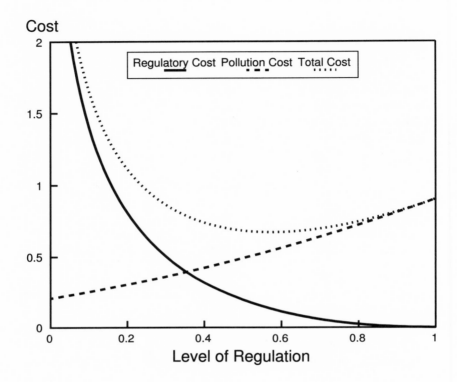

Figure 5.1: Cost of Various Regulatory Choices When Other Nations Hold Their Choices Fixed

However, as in other situations we have examined, there is a temptation to violate the agreement. For example, if states B and C each stick to the level 0.3732, then state A can benefit by regulating its industry less strictly (since it suffers all the cost of regulation but only some of the cost of pollution), with the most advantageous value being .5980. If A does this, then it reduces its cost from .6722 to .5640, but the costs of the other two states rise to .8107.

Another perspective on the model can be seen from Figure 5.2. The solid line in this model is the cost to A of varying regulatory choices, as in Figure 5.1, except that the other nations are assumed to be at the Nash level. The lack of individual incentive to change behavior can be seen from this. The broken line is the result of all three states changing their regulatory behavior in synchronization. This shows that the group incentives, in contrast to the individual incentives, can promote lower pollution emissions to the benefit of all, if the agreement holds.

5.2.1 Enforcement

In the absence of any observational error, a cooperative agreement, such as the optimal $(0.3732, 0.3732, 0.3732)$ one, can be enforced by a reversionary strategy. This would prescribe responding to a violation by reverting to the Nash equilibrium for some fixed period T and then returning to cooperation. The one-period cost of this agreement is .6722 to each state. Any state contemplating defection (for a one-period cost of .5640) would have to accept reversion to the Nash (for a one-period cost of .8261) for some number of periods T. The overall cost would be

$$.5640 + (\delta + \delta^2 + \cdots + \delta^T).8261 = .5640 + .8261(\delta - \delta^{T+1})/(1 - \delta),$$

which would be more costly than continuing the agreement, which has an overall cost of

$$.6722(1 - \delta^{T+1})/(1 - \delta),$$

whenever the punishment period T is sufficiently large, so long as the discount factor δ is larger than .41 (corresponding to an interest rate of 59 percent). Thus, under most circumstances the agreement could be enforced.

Since states A and B are contemplating the relative advantages of a two-state versus a three-state agreement, we need to pause and compare the benefits of the full agreement with those of the smaller one. It is the results of this choice, and not simply the typical calculation of whether it is in the best interests of a given state to cooperate or defect from an existing institution, that drives most of the subsequent analysis. The most beneficial two-state agreement is when A and B each regulate at .4434. State C is free to optimize against that value, yielding a regulatory value of .5773 for C. C then has a cost of .6627, better than the Nash (.8261) and the three-way cooperative agreement (.6722). States A and B have a cost of .7926, which is better than the Nash but not as good as the three-way cooperative agreement.

In this case of no uncertainty, states A and B prefer a multilateral agreement with all three states to a bilateral agreement because of the cost advantage. For the leader of C, things are more complicated. From the standpoint of cost alone, C's best strategy is to stay out and optimize against a bilateral agreement between A and B. However, we are assuming that the leader of C is willing to participate in the multilateral agreement because of the considerable prestige benefits associated with joining a trilateral institution.[4]

This analysis also highlights the fact that these environmental treaties do not completely correspond to the classic three-actor Prisoner's Dilemma. It is still the case that pure cooperation (one-period cost .6722) is more beneficial to all than pure defection (one-period cost .8261) and that there is a temptation for each state to defect (one-period cost to the defecting state .5640) while the others cooperate. However, two states benefit more from cooperating with each other and being exploited by the third (one-period cost .7926) than they would from defecting completely to the one-period Nash equilibrium (.8261).

5.2.2   Trigger Strategy

In this example, as in many others, the states know that there will be less than perfect information. States will not be able to observe the compliance levels of individual states and there is uncertainty with regard to any estimate of total emissions. These information uncertainties present a significant enforcement problem. Suppose that only the aggregate pollution level X can be estimated, and that this measurement is subject to errors with standard deviation σ (we use $\sigma = 0.1$ for illustration). As we saw in Chapter 4, a plausible method of enforcing such an agreement is a trigger strategy in which the agreement is abrogated if the measured pollution $\hat{X}_t$ at time t is greater than Π. This value Π is chosen to be greater than the agreed-upon level by an amount sufficient to account for uncertainty, while simultaneously providing enough disincentive to cheating to maintain the agreement.

As an example, suppose that a treaty calls for each state to limit its pollution to 0.45. This is a significant reduction from the Nash equilibrium level of about 0.55. The agreement is to be enforced by a threat to defect for three periods if the total pollution level is observed to be

---

[4]This might be represented in C's utility function as a onetime benefit in the period in which the trilateral agreement is concluded. This benefit is assumed to be large enough to overcome the modest cost differential between being a free rider and a full participant. It is also important in the subsequent story, since it provides an incentive for C to enter into an agreement, even if there is a substantial risk that it may be penalized for failing to be able to uphold it.

Cost

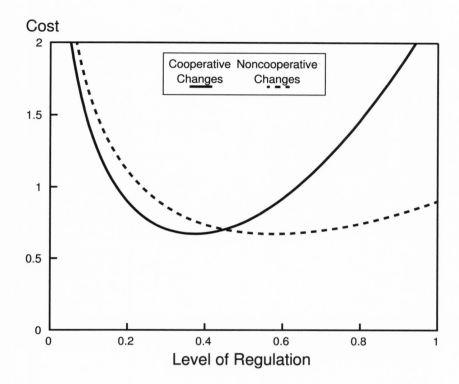

Figure 5.2: Cost of Various Regulatory Choices under Cooperative and Noncooperative Changes

higher than 1.4397 (1.4397 is .0897 higher than the total allowed pollution of 1.35; more formally, it is 0.897 standard deviations above the allowed pollution). Since the chance of a standard normal random variable exceeding .897 is 0.1849, this is the chance of an accidental violation occurring in any one period. The trigger level is chosen to eliminate an incentive for any nation to cheat by a small amount. If the trigger is exceeded and reversion occurs, it takes the form of each state being less vigilant in enforcing the de jure regulations on its own industry. Since a positive effort on the part of a government is required to maintain enforcement at a level sufficient to reduce emissions to the amounts stip-

ulated by the treaty, any decrease in enforcement enthusiasm is enough
to allow reversion.

If we use a discount rate of 10 percent the total (capitalized) cost
of noncooperation is 8.261 and the total cost of the treaty is 7.421, a
reduction in total cost of about 10 percent.[5] Note that one can quantify
the cost of uncertainty here by comparing the attendant costs of the
agreement (7.421) with the cost of such an agreement in the absence of
uncertainty (.7041/.10 = 7.041). An additional cost of uncertainty is
that the most cooperative agreement (at .3732) cannot be enforced by a
trigger strategy at all, so that this cost (6.722) cannot be achieved. Thus,
by one measure, the uncertainty inherent in the problem has increased
the overall costs by a factor of 7.421/6.722, which amounts to a 10
percent increase in costs.

As in the case without observational noise, we can compare the value
of an agreement between A and B only with one that involves all three
states. Such a two-state agreement would have A and B regulating at
level .45 in cooperative periods, with C free to act in an individually
optimal way. The cost of this trigger strategy equilibrium to A (or B)
is 7.783, which is better than the noncooperative Nash but not as good
as the results that can be obtained by the trilateral institution. In the
presence of observational errors alone, states A and B should invite state
C to join them in their agreement.

5.3 Capacity Uncertainty and Change

5.3.1 Capacity Uncertainty

Apart from having to cope with imperfect observation, states A and B
are concerned about the capacity β^C of state C to fulfill the terms of
the agreement. We will first examine the case in which this parameter
is stable over time but is uncertainly known at the time the treaty is
negotiated. We will then look at the more realistic but also analytically
more difficult case in which the parameter itself may change over time.

We will continue with the model and parameters of the last section,
and suppose that a treaty at 0.45 is contemplated. This treaty will be
enforced by a trigger strategy with trigger value $1.4397 = 3(.45) + .0894$

---

[5]The other way a trigger strategy equilibrium can fail is for one party to find it
profitable to abrogate the agreement completely and exploit the responses expected
from the other parties. One can check that such extreme exploitative behavior is not
profitable in this instance, yielding a cost to the exploiter of 7.814.

and a reversion period of 3. Suppose that nation C's β parameter, which we have been assuming is equal to 1, is uncertain. We will assume that the best estimate of this parameter is that its logarithm $\lambda^C = \log(\beta^C)$ is normally distributed with an expected value of 0 and a standard deviation of τ^C.

As usual, the trigger strategy equilibria that we are using specifies that the trigger should be chosen so that no state has an incentive to cheat. If state C has parameter $\beta^C = 1$, as assumed in the equilibrium calculations, then C will adhere to the enforcement requirements of the treaty, and the cost to state A or B will be 7.421. If β^C is larger than 1, then C will have an incentive to cut down on enforcement, since it is more difficult for C than was acknowledged in the treaty; if $\beta^C < 1$, then the reverse will be true. The overall effect can be seen if we examine values of β^C that are 10 percent above and 10 percent below the nominal value of 1. The effect of this on nation A or B is that the cost increases to 7.555 or decreases to 7.284, respectively. If there is an equal chance of either deviation, then the expected value is $(7.555 + 7.284)/2 = 7.420$; this differs only marginally from the value with no deviations. Thus such uncertainty really has little or no cost to the other parties to the treaty. This is true because for small amounts of uncertainty, the payoff function is almost linear, so that the expectation of the payoff is about equal to the payoff at the expectation; therefore uncertainty does not matter. This is illustrated in Figure 5.3, which shows the near linearity of A's utility function with changes in C's capacity parameter.

However, the situation changes if the uncertainty about β^C is sufficiently large. Then there is a possibility that state C's capacity may be so poor that it may actually abrogate the treaty, at considerable cost to all participants. This cost comes from states A and B having to forgo the benefits of a bilateral treaty to enforce the trilateral treaty. With the parameter values we have been using, the critical point is where $\beta^C = 1.540$; for treaties that are more cooperative than the one we have been examining, the danger point will be closer to the nominal value, and this means that if τ^C, the uncertainty in β^C, is large enough, there will be a nonnegligible chance that the treaty may fall apart immediately. Since this would have a high cost if it occurred, and since the chance of this unpleasant event is not balanced by any similarly probable positive event, it provides a disincentive for A and B to include C in the treaty, when it would otherwise be a close decision. This situation is illustrated in Figure 5.4, which shows the large drop in A's utility when

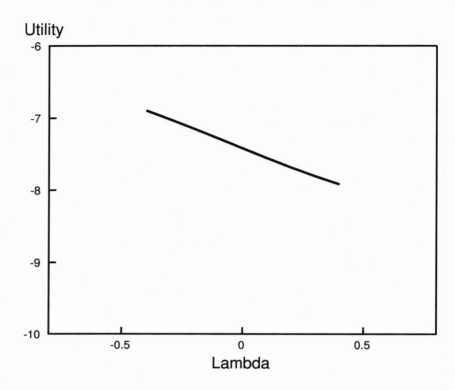

Figure 5.3: Payoff to State A as a Function of State C's Capacity Parameter β^C for Small-to-Moderate Changes in β^C

C's capacity parameter exceeds the point at which the agreement can no longer be enforced in any manner. If such changes are at all probable, capacity uncertainty will have had a strong negative effect on A's utility that must be considered.

Note that the consequences of defecting from a treaty grow worse and more likely as the treaty becomes more deeply cooperative. One implication of this is that capacity uncertainty operates to limit the treaty's depth of cooperation. New institutions that include a heterogeneous group of states that vary with respect to capacity are unlikely to generate large amounts of cooperation. Moreover, only to the extent that such capacity is reduced can we expect existing institutions to become more deeply cooperative over time.

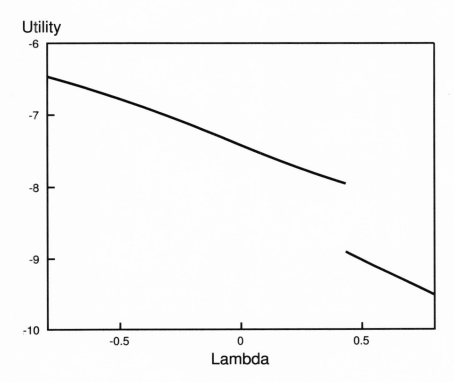

Figure 5.4: Payoff to State A as a Function of State C's Capacity Parameter β^C for Large Changes in β^C

5.3.2 Capacity Change

Recall, however, that states A and B are uncertain not simply about state C's present capacity to implement the agreement, but also about how that capacity might change over time. As the introduction suggests, this concern is not unusual. There is no question that state capacity can change over time and that the direction of change is uncertain. To capture this phenomenon, we will add two features to the model. First, C's behavior at each turn adds some information about the true value of the parameter β^C. Second, the value of β^C changes in each period.

First, consider how an observation of C's behavior may affect A's (or B's) knowledge of C's capacity parameter. The current state of knowledge of A or B about $\lambda^C = \log(\beta^C)$ can be represented by a normal distribution with mean ξ_t^C and variance $(\tau_t^C)^2$ (written $N(\xi_t^C, (\tau_t^C)^2)$). In each period A and B observe the pollution level X, which provides an estimate of λ^C that can be treated as approximately normal with standard deviation $\tilde{\sigma}$ (this will be a multiple of the observation standard deviation σ that depends on the function that transforms an observation of pollution level into an estimate of λ^C). Thus, we treat X_t as drawn from $N(\lambda_t, \tilde{\sigma}^2)$. We can then update our knowledge of λ_t using Bayes' rule to obtain the posterior distribution

$$N\left(\frac{\xi_t(\tau_t^C)^{-2} + x_t\tilde{\sigma}^{-2}}{(\tau_t^C)^{-2} + \tilde{\sigma}^{-2}}, \frac{1}{(\tau_t^C)^{-2} + \tilde{\sigma}^{-2}} \right).$$

Otherwise expressed, we have

$$\xi_{t+1}^C = \frac{\xi_t^C(\tau_t^C)^{-2} + x_t\tilde{\sigma}^{-2}}{(\tau_t^C)^{-2} + \tilde{\sigma}^{-2}} \tag{5.2}$$

$$(\tau_{t+1}^C)^2 = \frac{1}{(\tau_t^C)^{-2} + \tilde{\sigma}^{-2}}. \tag{5.3}$$

Now we add to the model the second new factor: a change that occurs each period in the parameter that is being estimated. This adds to the model as follows:

$$X_t = \lambda_t^C + \eta_t \tag{5.4}$$

$$\lambda_{t+1}^C = \lambda_t + \epsilon_{t+1} \tag{5.5}$$

$$\lambda_0^C \sim N(\zeta_0, \tau_0^2) \tag{5.6}$$

$$\eta_t \sim N(0, \tilde{\sigma}^2) \tag{5.7}$$

$$\epsilon_t \sim N(0, \upsilon^2) \tag{5.8}$$

We then have a standard state-space model (Hannan and Deistler 1988; Harvey 1981; Jazwinski 1970; Pole, West, and Harrison 1988; West and Harrison 1989). If we add this change to the posterior distribution derived above, we find that $\lambda_{t+1}^C \sim N(\xi_{t+1}^C, (\tau_{t+1}^C)^2)$ where the updating formula (5.2) is unchanged but the updating formula for the variance becomes[6]

$$(\tau_{t+1}^C)^2 = \frac{1}{(\tau_t^C)^{-2} + \tilde{\sigma}^{-2}} + \upsilon^2. \tag{5.9}$$

---

[6]If this is compared with the formula in Theorem (2.3) in West and Harrison (1989), the differences are due to the fact that they take as the fundamental aspect of the problem the posterior distribution of β_t after the information is collected, whereas the nature of our problem dictates that it is the prior distribution of β_{t+1} which is relevant.

An important descriptive parameter for our model is the signal-to-noise ratio $\rho = v^2/\tilde{\sigma}^2$. Here $\tilde{\sigma}^2$ is the observational error variance, and v^2 is the variance of the period-to-period changes in the parameter. If the signal-to-noise ratio is large (much greater than 1), then our information about the change is instantaneously updated to a high degree of accuracy; this results in the irreducible minimum of uncertainty about the other side. If, however, ρ is small (much less than 1), then a substantial amount of additional uncertainty is added by measurement or observational problems.[7]

5.3.3 Equilibrium Behavior

The transient behavior of the model of capacity change and information acquisition can be very complex, but fortunately an equilibrium is usually quickly reached in which the information lost by a potential change in the parameter is just balanced by the information gained in each period. The equilibrium provides a convenient way to examine the effects of two variables on the long-run uncertainty about an opponent's capacity. The first is v, the standard deviation of one-period changes in the opponent's capacity (literally, the standard deviation of changes in a parameter λ that influences the opponent's capacity). The second is the standard deviation $\tilde{\sigma}$ of the information derived in each period about the opponent's capacity.

Suppose for simplicity that both the variance σ^2 of the information added and the variance v^2 of the change in the parameter β are constant.[8] Then the sequence of variances of β_t converges to a value τ_0^2 satisfying the equation

$$\tau_0^2 = \frac{1}{\tau_0^{-2} + \sigma^{-2}} + v^2$$

---

[7]There are two limiting cases that deserve mention. If $\tilde{\sigma}_t = 0$, so that perfect information is derived about the value of β at time t, then, in the limit, $\xi_{t+1}^C = x_t = \lambda_t$ and $(\tau_{t+1}^C)^2 = v_{t+1}^2$. In this case the only uncertainty is the period-to-period change, which is instantly appraised. If $\tilde{\sigma}_t = \infty$, so that no new information is derived about the value of β at time t, then, in the limit, $\xi_{t+1}^C = \xi_t^C$ and $(\tau_{t+1}^C)^2 = (\tau_t^C)^2 + v_{t+1}^2$ This model implies that information about the opponent becomes progressively worse over time, without bound. Because these two cases are both uninteresting and unrealistic, we assume from now on that $\tilde{\sigma}_t$ is finite and nonzero.

[8]If the variances σ^2 and v^2 vary randomly from period to period, then this amounts to an assumption that the distributions of X and ϵ are mixtures of normals instead of normal (Appendix 5.7.1), and this can be accommodated into the Bayesian updating procedure at the risk of some extra complexity (Titterington, Smith and Makov 1985; Everitt and Hand 1981). We will stick for the moment to the normality assumption since it makes the analysis somewhat more tractable. However, this assumption is not a requirement to use the models that we are describing.

$$0 = \tau_0^4 - v^2\tau_0^2 - v^2\sigma^2$$

which is a quadratic equation in τ_0^2 having solution

$$\begin{aligned}
\tau_0^2 &= 0.5v(v + \sqrt{v^2 + 4\sigma^2}) \\
&= 0.5v^2(1 + \sqrt{1 + 4/\rho})
\end{aligned}$$

The convergence follows from Theorem 2.3 in West and Harrison (1989) or can easily be proved directly by showing the contractive nature of the iteration (5.9). This also has the side benefit of showing that the sequence of variances τ_t^2 moves monotonically to the limit with the distance being reduced at each iteration by at least the factor $\sigma^2/(\sigma^2 + \tau_0^2)$.

Figure 5.5 shows a contour plot of τ_0 against σ and v. It is apparent that the long-run uncertainty τ_0 increases as either σ or v increase, but that the standard deviation v of the change in β has a much larger effect than does the standard deviation σ of the information X acquired about β.

Since τ_0 changes proportionately if both σ and v are multiplied by any factor, another way to examine this relationship is in terms of $\rho = v^2/\sigma^2$, while fixing $v = 1$. Some values of σ ($= 1/\sqrt{\rho}$ in this case) and the resulting values of τ_0 are shown in Figure 5.6. It is clear that reducing σ (the information uncertainty) to very low levels ($\rho \to \infty$) results in the only uncertainty being due to v. Very large values of σ ($\rho \to 0$) cause great uncertainty, although not as great as v itself.

In sum, both factors affect the long-run uncertainty, but the size of the changes (v) is considerably more important than the errors in information derived (σ). This is true because the effect of observational uncertainty is greatly diminished after a relatively short period of time. The effect of the changes in the parameter β^C persists indefinitely, however. *This finding suggests that a good deal of the importance that people attribute to capacity uncertainty is actually the product of fears that state capacity might change over time in unexpected and possibly costly ways.*[9]

---

[9]If there were no change at all in the parameter β^C, A and B's knowledge would increase over time, until there was no uncertainty left; under these conditions capacity uncertainty would be ephemeral. Yet this flies in the face of considerable experience that suggests that uncertainties about the capabilities (and preferences) of other nations persist over time, even in the face of frequent interaction.

Changes Standard Deviation

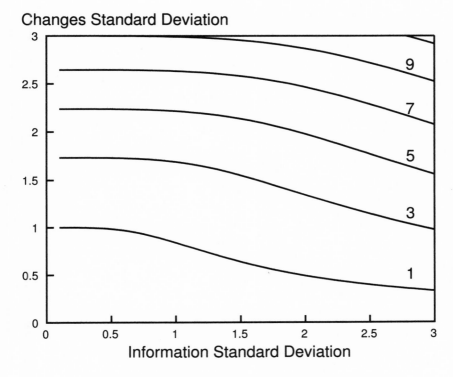

Figure 5.5: Determinants of Long-Run Uncertainty

5.4 The Effects of State Capacity Uncertainty

We have seen that the main problem caused by capacity uncertainty is that, if the unknown capacity parameter passes a given threshold, then the treaty will fall apart. Furthermore, the prospect of this happening is a deterrent to entering into the treaty to begin with. We have so far examined this effect only in a qualitative way. In order to obtain a more quantitative estimate of this effect, we will use a somewhat simplified model.

This model has C's capacity take on only two values, corresponding to a cooperative regime and a noncooperative regime. This is reasonable,

Standard Deviation

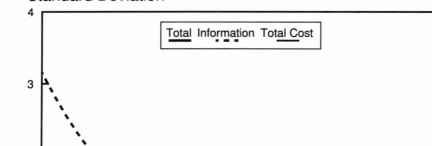

Figure 5.6: τ_0 and σ a Function of ρ When $v = 1$

since the variation in behavior within each regime is much smaller than the behavior between regimes. Specifically, we assume the two values are $\beta^C = 1$ and $\beta^C = \bar{\beta}^C$, the latter value being above the threshold of agreement abrogation. Let p_0 be the prior probability that $\beta^C = 1$, according to A and B's information before entering the agreement. If A or B wishes to assess the merits of the agreement, then A and B must consider that C might immediately abrogate the treaty (i.e., $\beta^C = \bar{\beta}^C$). In addition, we model the potential secular change in β^C by assuming that there is a fixed probability π that β^C will change from 1 to $\bar{\beta}^C$ in a given period. Once that happens, the treaty will be lost.

To calculate the value of this outcome, let c_0 be the cost to A or B of one period of the treaty (allowing that this may consist of cooperation or reversion, depending on past behavior). Let c_1 be value to A or B of an abrogated agreement. Let Π be the matrix

$$\begin{pmatrix} \pi & 0 \\ 1 - \pi & 1 \end{pmatrix}$$

let P be the vector $(p_0, 1 - p_0)^\top$, let $C = (c_0, c_1)$, and let δ be the discount factor. Then the value of the treaty is

$$\begin{aligned} V &= C(I + \Pi\delta + \Pi^2\delta^2 + \cdots)P \\ &= C(I - \Pi\delta)^{-1}P. \end{aligned} \tag{5.10}$$

Some numerical values we can apply to this come from the previous examples. The per period cost of the treaty is .7420, and the per period cost of abrogation is .8903. If the prior probability of $\beta^C = 1$ is $p_0 = .9$, then the value of the treaty would seem to be $.7420(.9) + .8903(.1) = .7569$, which is a far better outcome than remaining at the Nash (whose value is .8261 per period). However, this does not account for the potential change in capacity, as (5.10) does. If we add a probability of changing from $\beta^C = 1$ to $\beta^C = \bar{\beta}^C$ of $\pi = .12$, then (5.10) yields $V = .8262$, slightly worse than remaining at the Nash.

In previous sections we learned that a sufficiently large amount of capacity uncertainty and capacity change would make the prospect of entering into an institution with a new state unattractive. From this illustration, we learn that even relatively modest doubts about the current capabilities of a potential treaty partner, combined with a relatively modest chance of a change in capabilities that would undermine the treaty, can destroy the incentive to create a multilateral institution.

5.5 Informational Issue-Linking and a Multivariate Model

One possible way to reduce the impact of capacity uncertainty in an area such as environmental regulation is by adding information from other policy areas. Environmental regulation is, after all, a relatively recent phenomenon, and information about state capacity in this arena is relatively scarce. It is only logical to wonder whether that capacity estimate can be improved by drawing upon the history of a state's performance in other areas. In order to explore the extent to which this is possible, we will outline an extension of the theory of this chapter to this multivariate context. With p policy areas under simultaneous consideration, we need to expand the capacity parameter to a p-vector in which there is one component for each area. Observations that will be used to update knowledge of this p-dimensional parameter will also be multidimensional, and we will explore the effects that correlations among these different areas have on the ability to import information from one policy area to another.

Let Θ_t be a p-vector parameter of unknown characteristics of an opponent. We assume that the state of knowledge at time t is represented by $\Theta_t \sim N(\Xi_t, T_t)$, where Ξ_t is a p-vector representing the best guess as to the value of Θ_t and T_t is the $p \times p$ covariance matrix of the prior distribution. Assume that an observation X_t is drawn from $N(\Theta_t, \Sigma)$. Then the posterior distribution of Θ_t is

$$N([\Sigma^{-1} + T_t^{-1}]^{-1}[\Sigma^{-1}x_t + T_t^{-1}\Xi_t], [\Sigma^{-1} + T_t^{-1}]^{-1}).$$

If Θ is also subject to change over time, represented by $\Theta_{t+1} = \Theta_t + E_t$, where $E \sim N(0, \Upsilon)$, then the revised distribution is $\Theta_{t+1} \sim N(\Xi_{t+1}, T_{t+1})$ where

$$
\begin{aligned}
\Xi_{t+1} &= [\Sigma^{-1} + T_t^{-1}]^{-1}[\Sigma^{-1}x_t + T^{-1}\Xi_t] \\
T_{t+1} &= [\Sigma^{-1} + T_t^{-1}]^{-1} + \Upsilon.
\end{aligned}
$$

This process has a fixed point to which it converges as the following proposition shows. This is a multivariate generalization of Theorem 2.3 in West and Harrison (1989; see also section 15.2).

Proposition 5.1 *Let Σ, Υ, and T be positive definite symmetric (PDS) matrices and define the matrix function $f()$ by*

$$f(T) = \left(\Sigma^{-1} + T^{-1}\right)^{-1} + \Upsilon.$$

Then f is a contraction.

PROOF. See Appendix 5.7.2

Imagine that we are considering using information from the area of trade relations to derive information about environmental capacity β_S. Some experimentation shows that the critical factors are the signal-to-noise ratio of the environmental parameter ($\rho_S = \upsilon_S/\sigma_S$), the correlation between changes in the environmental parameter and changes in the trade parameter (γ_υ), and the correlation between observational errors in the environmental and trade arenas (γ_σ). In what follows we take the variance of the changes to be one for both environment and trade, since the results are invariant to the choice of these factors.

First, if ρ_S is large, then the information gained about β_S from the sequence of observations on environmental action is nearly as good as is feasible—the uncertainty can never fall below v_S. For example, with $\rho_S = 10$, we do not need external information since $\tau_S = 1.004$, very near the bound of 1.0. However, if ρ_S is small, meaning that information about the opponent's environmental parameter is seriously lacking, then there is the potential for another area to assist.

It turns out that the most favorable condition for using information about trade to make inferences about the environment parameter is when γ_σ and γ_v are both large in magnitude and of opposite signs. This means that we need another area whose parameter tends to move with the environmental parameter, but with observational errors that are negatively correlated (or vice versa). In such cases, very large improvements can be made. For example, if $\rho_S = .1$, $\gamma_\sigma = -.9$ and $\gamma_v = .9$, then the uncertainty τ_S is reduced by 53 percent. If the two correlations are of magnitude .99, then the reduction reaches 80 percent. Even in less extreme cases, use of a second field can reduce uncertainty. If the parameter movements are correlated with $\gamma_v = .9$ but observational errors are independent, the reduction in uncertainty is 14 percent.

These results suggest that there are times when capacity information can be imported from one policy area to another to reduce uncertainty. However, the requirements to do so are quite strict: correlations need to be very high and of opposite signs. In many cases, these requirements will not be met or the extent to which they are satisfied will be unknown. In a way, this justifies the common modeling practice of considering only one policy area at a time.

5.6   Conclusion

In this chapter, we have modeled how uncertainty about state capacity affects the membership of an institution designed to regulate pollution. Two states that border a common body of water are faced with the choice of creating either a bilateral agreement or a trilateral institution that includes a third state. The states are uncertain about the capacity of the third, less economically developed state to implement the agreement's regulatory provisions within its borders, and they worry that its capacity may deteriorate in the future.

We found that small amounts of uncertainty about the third state's capacity had almost no effect on either the stability of the treaty or its ex ante attractiveness. This continues to be true until there is a real possibility that the state's incapacity will be such that it will immediately be judged to be in noncompliance with the agreement. Hence, if a state's present capacity to implement the institution's norms is the only thing at issue, it will usually make sense to ignore that fact and offer it membership in the institution.

When uncertainty is introduced with regard to the state's future capacity—reflected in changes in its capacity parameter—the situation is quite different. Even relatively modest amounts of uncertainty about a state's present and future capacity can make highly cooperative treaties too risky to undertake. In the context of the environmental treaty, this risk stems less from the fear of exploitation—as it might in an area such as arms control—than from the realization that punishment is costly. In this case, every time the third state violates the treaty, the other two states are forced to suspend the cooperation between them to punish it.

One might respond that this situation is quite unusual and is relevant largely to a small subset of cartel-like institutions where overproduction or its equivalent represents the only enforcement strategy. If the agreement were enforced by some sort of sanction or linkage strategy, could not the two states proceed with their bilateral cooperation while punishing the third state? The answer is yes, but it may be more difficult than it appears. Our admittedly limited observations of interstate regulatory institutions suggest that domestic constituencies get extremely upset when they find themselves being held to a regulatory standard that other states have not implemented. Cries of "unfair to U.S. industry" and "all we ask for is a level playing field" are often a prelude to reduced regulatory enforcement. Moreover, the fact that there will be instances when a linkage strategy punishment is possible does not negate the fact that punishment is still costly. Even if it is available, there will be a point, granted a higher point, at which uncertainty about state capacity and capacity change makes a small multilateral institution that works well preferable to a larger multilateral institution that requires a choice between constant enforcement battles and a reduced level of regulatory enforcement.

Of course, different states may have very different ideas about what is preferable. This chapter has been written largely from the perspective of two states trying to decide whether or not to invite a third, less capable state, to join their regulatory regime. The third state's preferences have been largely ignored, except insofar as we have assumed that its leadership is motivated to join the regime by one-time prestige benefit. We believe that this accurately characterizes the motivations of some developing states, but our findings have important implications for those states whose motivations are much darker. For example, suppose the leader of state C saw few prestige benefits associated with a regime, but believed that it was quite likely that it would, over the course of time, evolve in the direction of increasingly strict regulation. Realizing the role that enforcement costs play in determining the depth of cooperation, he or she might well have an incentive to join the regime for no other reason than to slow this rate of evolution. The magnitude of this incentive depends, of course, on the nature of the regime. State C would obviously fear the rapid evolution of a trade or security regime that excluded it more than it would fear the rapid evolution of an environmental regime because the costs of exclusion from the former would be much higher.

5.7 Appendixes

5.7.1 Normal Mixture Distributions

Suppose that a random variable X_i has distribution $N(\mu, \sigma_i^2)$, where σ_i^2 is itself randomly sampled from a distribution $m(x)$. Then X is said to be a scale mixture of normals. The density of X is given by

$$f_X(x) = \int_0^\infty \phi(x; \mu, \sigma^2) m(x) \, dx,$$

where $\phi(x; \mu, \sigma^2)$ is the normal density function. These distributions are all symmetric. An appeal to Jensen's inequality shows that they are also all longer tailed than the normal, in the sense of having a higher standardized fourth moment. Many standard symmetric distributions can be written as normal scale mixtures, including the t-distributions.

5.7.2 Proof of Proposition 5.1

Note that $f(T)$ is also clearly PDS, since the sums and inverses of PDS matrices are PDS. Let T and T_0 be arbitrary PDS matrices. We have

$$
\begin{aligned}
f(T) - f(T_0) &= \left(\Sigma^{-1} + T^{-1}\right)^{-1} + \Upsilon - \left(\Sigma^{-1} + T_0^{-1}\right)^{-1} - \Upsilon \\
&= \left(\Sigma^{-1} + T^{-1}\right)^{-1} - \left(\Sigma^{-1} + T_0^{-1}\right)^{-1}.
\end{aligned}
$$

So

$$
\begin{aligned}
(\Sigma^{-1} + T^{-1})(f(T) - f(T_0))(\Sigma^{-1} + T_0^{-1}) &= (\Sigma^{-1} + T_0^{-1}) \\
&\quad - (\Sigma^{-1} + T^{-1}) \\
&= T_0^{-1} - T^{-1} \\
(T\Sigma^{-1} + I)(f(T) - f(T_0))(\Sigma^{-1}T_0 + I) &= T - T_0.
\end{aligned}
$$

Now, using the usual matrix norm

$$
\|A\| = \max_x \frac{\|Ax\|}{\|x\|}
$$

we have

$$
\|T\Sigma^{-1} + I\| \cdot \|\Sigma\| = \|T + \Sigma\| > \|\Sigma\|
$$

because Σ and T are PDS so

$$
\|T\Sigma^{-1} + I\| > 1.
$$

Thus

$$
\begin{aligned}
\|f(T) - f(T_0)\| &= \|T\Sigma^{-1} + I\|^{-1} \cdot \|\Sigma^{-1}T_0 + I\|^{-1} \cdot \|T - T_0\| \\
&< \|T - T_0\|,
\end{aligned}
$$

as required.   □

It is possible to say something more about the fixed point to which this process converges. To derive the fixed point for this process, note that the matrix equation

$$
\begin{aligned}
(AX - B)'(AX - B) &= C \\
X'A'AX - B'AX - X'A'B + B'B - C &= 0,
\end{aligned}
$$

has a solution given by $X = A^{-1}(QC^{1/2} + B)$, where the exponent $1/2$ indicates the Cholesky factor and Q is any orthogonal matrix. The fixed point satisfies the equation

$$
\begin{aligned}
T &= [\Sigma^{-1} + T^{-1}]^{-1} + \Upsilon \\
T\Sigma^{-1} + I &= I + \Upsilon\Sigma^{-1} + \Upsilon T^{-1} \\
T\Sigma^{-1}T &= \Upsilon\Sigma^{-1}T + \Upsilon \\
0 &= T\Sigma^{-1}T - \Upsilon\Sigma^{-1}T - \Upsilon.
\end{aligned}
$$

Since also

$$0 \; = \; T\Sigma^{-1}T - T\Sigma^{-1}\Upsilon - \Upsilon$$

we have

$$0 \; = \; T\Sigma^{-1}T - 0.5\Upsilon\Sigma^{-1}T - 0.5T\Sigma^{-1}\Upsilon - \Upsilon.$$

Identifying terms, we have

$$
\begin{aligned}
A'A &= \Sigma^{-1} \\
B'A &= 0.5\Upsilon\Sigma^{-1} \\
B'B - C &= -\Upsilon
\end{aligned}
$$

so that

$$
\begin{aligned}
A &= Q_1\Sigma^{-1/2} \\
B' &= 0.5\Upsilon\Sigma^{-1}A^{-1} \\
&= 0.5\Upsilon A' \\
C &= B'B + \Upsilon \\
&= 0.25\Upsilon A'A\Upsilon + \Upsilon \\
&= 0.25\Upsilon\Sigma^{-1}\Upsilon + \Upsilon
\end{aligned}
$$

Hence,

$$
\begin{aligned}
T &= A^{-1}(Q_2 C^{1/2} + B) \\
&= A^{-1}Q_2 C^{1/2} + 0.5\Upsilon \\
&= \Sigma^{1/2}Q_1'Q_2 C^{1/2} + 0.5\Upsilon
\end{aligned}
$$

where the orthogonal matrices Q_1 and Q_2 are such that the fixed point is symmetric.

Chapter 6
Conclusion

Without measureless and perpetual uncertainty the drama of human life
would be destroyed.
—Winston Churchill

6.1 Domestic Uncertainty and Institutions

The Pandora's box of uncertainties connected with domestic politics affect international relations in many ways. Especially important is the
shaping of international and domestic institutions that, in turn, influence the character of the international system. Just as uncertainty about
medical diagnoses leads to such institutions as second opinions and malpractice insurance, so a constituency's uncertainty about the motives of
its elected officials leads to institutions such as legislative approval for
declarations of war and the voter decision rule that calls for the removal
of a leader who fails to achieve victory for whatever reason.

These institutions are interesting because they represent, at least
in part, endogenous adaptations to the fact of uncertainty. That is,
they exist because actors know that uncertainty will have an impact on
their ability to accomplish their goals and they want to minimize its
ill effects. This is not to argue that the nature of every institutional
decision rule that has an impact on international relations is determined
solely by domestic uncertainty. Institutions, after all, are affected by a
host of distributive concerns and other transaction costs. Yet even the
few examples described in this book should be enough to convince the
reader that domestic uncertainty often plays a surprisingly important
role in determining the nature of international institutions.

When institutions are treated as exogenous and part of the strategic
environment, as they are in most research traditions, every institutional

adaptation that takes place because of uncertainty is also considered to be exogenous. Ironically, the more that uncertainty shapes institutions, the more its effects will tend to be concealed. For example, uncertainty about a doctor's local reputation will mean less in a medical care system that has board certification, malpractice insurance, and second opinions than in one that does not. If we fail to see these institutions as a response to uncertainty, we will underestimate the effect that it has had on the system.

In an analogous way, uncertainty about a state's political commitment to the principles of arms control will appear to matter less when a treaty calls for on-site inspection and when the other signatories have credibly committed themselves to strong sanctions than when these uncertainty-inspired institutions are absent. If we ignore the initial rationale for creating these institutions and try to estimate the impact of domestic uncertainty when they are present, we will also underestimate its effects. To avoid falling prey to this inferential trap, one must pause to consider whether an institution would exist in the form it does (i.e., whether its structure and decision rules would be the same) if domestic uncertainty were not a problem. Whenever the answer is no, uncertainty matters.

The only way to appreciate the influence that domestic uncertainty has on the international system via its effect on institutions (including the prevention of their establishment) is to acknowledge the existence of domestic uncertainty at the outset and model its effects. Chapter 3 began with the recognition that voters are uncertain about (1) whether their executive's preferences about when conflict should be initiated or continued are the same as their own and (2) the extent to which the information they have been given about the benefits and costs of military action reflect what the executive actually knows to be the case. We then examined how these two domestic uncertainties influence the international system through their effect on democracy's most fundamental institution, the election. Not only is the problem substantively important in a society that continues to speculate about the degree of misrepresentation involved in Vietnam and the Iran-Contra Affair, but it also represents a sharp departure from the unitary actor model which critics wrongly believe is as intrinsic to formal modeling as it is to structural realism.

Using a principal-agent model, we investigated how a constituency can most effectively employ the reelection sanction to deter executives from exploiting their information advantage to initiate conflict in a manner that is inconsistent with the preferences of the median voter. We showed first that when the executive's information advantages are great (i.e., the constituency possesses no reliable and independent source of benefit and cost data about the conflict), uncertainty forces the constituency to base its retention decision on the outcome of the conflict rather than on its ex ante advisability. The basic decision rule is that if an executive initiates an unsuccessful war, he or she must be voted out of office. Should the constituency fail to do this, it will be proffering an invitation to future executives to exploit their information advantage and act on the basis of their own preferences rather than on those of voters.

Unfortunately, as the title of this book suggests, any institutional strategy for coping with uncertainty has attendant costs. Because the constituency cannot distinguish between a bad outcome that was caused by a decision that it would not support and an outcome that results from nothing more than unforeseeable events, the constituency is forced to remove effective but unlucky executives who made the best possible decision in a difficult case. Most readers, if not most officeholders, are likely to consider this a modest cost. Part of the price of political ambition has always been having to take the blame for events such as recessions that are not of one's making.

A greater cost stems from the fact that the harsh practice of dismissing unsuccessful executives creates an incentive for those connected with an unsuccessful war effort to "gamble for resurrection" by escalating or prolonging a conflict that voters would like to terminate. The dynamic is the same that drives a savings and loan executive who has made some unsuccessful investments and faces dismissal when the yearly audit is conducted. Given that dismissal is inevitable and no worse punishment is likely, she decides to invest still more money in still riskier investments, hoping to recoup the losses and save her job. The catch is that because the new loans are riskier than the old ones, the chances of their failing is even greater and a bad situation is (on average) made worse.

The practical implications of this are several. One is that the more zealous a constituency is in guarding against exploitation by punishing unsuccessful executives, the more it must guard against gambling for resurrection. The same penalty for failure that deters an aggressive executive can entrap an unlucky executive who intervenes appropriately but has the misfortune of presiding over higher than expected casualties. Whether guilty or innocent the executives facing the prospect of near certain electoral defeat are led to adopt riskier strategies. Another implication is that parliamentary forms of government should, ceteris paribus, witness less gambling for resurrection behavior than presidential systems. The advantage has nothing to do with the relative efficiency of the two forms of government. It is simply that the fixed terms associated with a presidential system will often give the executive more time to experiment with risky strategies.

How frequently does gambling for resurrection actually occur in losing conflicts? To answer the question adequately would obviously require the analysis of a large number of cases in which difficult variables like an executive's chances of reelection and the risk associated with different military decisions were accurately measured. We possess no such data. However, we did examine a recent volume edited by Levite et al. (1992) that contained case studies of unsuccessful interventions—a context in which the model predicts that gambling for resurrection will occur. There we discovered evidence in support of two predictions made by the theory: (1) in every case, executives who initiate losing interventions take steps to prolong or escalate them longer than their constituencies—who first supported the interventions—appeared to desire; and (2) no executive who initiated a losing effort attempted to withdraw, although their successors frequently did so.

Finally, there is nothing inherent in the theory underlying the model that would limit the problem of gambling for resurrection to conflict situations. The incentives that drive it will be present whenever a constituency is forced—because of its information disadvantage and its suspicion of executive motives—to judge an executive's decisions more by results than by ex ante advisability. This extends the generalizability of the phenomenon to other critical areas of public policy, for example, fiscal policy.

Thus, a constituency that throws out an executive who presides over a recession may be doing more than punishing an incompetent. The constituency may be relying on economic performance to keep executives from manipulating the economic policy to serve favored special interests. Our theory, therefore, can be seen as receiving modest support from the findings of researchers who have studied the propensity of executives to divert attention from poor economic performance by engaging in foreign wars (Hess and Orphanides 1994; Smith 1994). It also raises the possibility that executives may gamble with even riskier fiscal policies, as well as foreign adventures. The particular avenue an executive selects will depend on the size of the payoff and the transaction costs (e.g., the necessity and likelihood of legislative approval) involved.

Chapter 4 demonstrated how uncertainty about the nature of interest group demands operates to shape the enforcement strategy embodied in the GATT and Super 301. The analysis began by determining how a free trade regime should be enforced in the absence of any complicating factors. The choice of enforcement strategy is shown to depend on the temptation to defect, which rises with variations in the restrictiveness or cooperativeness of the particular agreement. The deeper the cooperation represented by the agreement, the harsher the punishment required to support it. It follows that if an agreement requires a significant decrease in tariff levels (i.e., if the level of cooperation embodied in the agreement is high), a relatively harsh punishment will be required to prevent violations.

The GATT appears to ignore this reasoning. Instead of prescribing a punishment harsh enough to cancel out the benefits of defection, the GATT formalizes the much weaker "compensation principle," which requires the violator to reduce tariffs an equivalent amount in another area. If no such compensation is offered, the victim state may withdraw a level of benefits from the violator (i.e., reintroduce tariffs) equivalent to the injury suffered. Although this principle of compensation embodies a defensible notion of fairness, the fact that the level of redress is calibrated by the amount of injury done to the victim rather than by the benefits that violation provides the violator guarantees that it will not function as an effective deterrent. Why implement such a system?

We showed that what appears to be a perversely suboptimal solution to the problem of maintaining free trade actually provides governments with the opportunity to reap greater benefits by satisfying the periodic demands of domestic constituencies. Uncertainty enters the picture in the form of a lack of predictability about the precise nature and timing of the demands. Were the uncertainty absent, the demands would be incorporated into the basic agreement at the outset, as are the exceptions connected with agriculture. The compensation principle allows opportunistic exceptions but acts to keep the system from breaking down. It does this by setting the equivalent of a "fine" for violations that prevents excessive violations and coordinates expectations about what will happen in the event that a state breaks the rules. In short, the attractiveness of this close relative of Tit-for-Tat springs from both its weaknesses and its strengths.

A second asymmetric model produced the less intuitive result that the system is not supported solely by each state's expectation that it will periodically want to violate the treaty. Even if a particular state is confident that it will never want to defect from a standard of complete free trade, it will not necessarily lobby for the adoption of more severe penalties for violations. This is because other governments that receive notable constituency benefits will decide that it still pays to defect under the new rules—even if it pays somewhat less than before. A free trade state that ignores this fact may find that any benefits of a more restrictive treaty are more than offset by the increased costs of having to punish a greater number of violations.

The constituency benefits that flow from the ability to defect periodically lead us to view Section 301 and even Super 301 not so much as attempts to increase the level of cooperation embodied in the GATT (i.e., by increasing its restrictiveness) as efforts to extend the GATT principles into related areas that had not been covered. This is especially true in the case of nontariff barriers (NTBs) that present states with the seductive option of being able to violate the spirit of the treaty without paying any compensation.

Evidence suggests that these laws did, in fact, play such a role. Notwithstanding the criticism that Section 301 embodies the principal of "harsh unilateralism," the retaliation that it has inspired has been neither harsh nor frequently applied (Bayard and Elliott 1994). Indeed, its language on retaliation mimics the comparatively mild and interest group sensitive compensation principle found in the GATT (Sykes 1991–92). It should come as no surprise then that the use of Section 301 and Super 301 failed to provoke the kind of trade wars that its more pessimistic critics had predicted.

The other side of the coin is that neither the use of Section 301 nor the operation of the new GATT rules that it inspired are likely to ward off occasional defections in the future. However successful these rules are in extending free trade into new areas, they still do not provide for punishments that are nearly harsh enough to prevent periodic violations in response to uncertain interest group demand. These will continue until the political benefits provided by interests groups are no longer larger than the corresponding political costs that politicians have to endure when they face a compensation principle-defined penalty.

As long as there are interest groups that can reap benefits from transient protection, neither moment is likely to come soon. There are few states where such interest groups are so without resources that they cannot, in time of crisis, compensate a chief executive with resources that are well above the level she needs to absorb the political heat associated with a much delayed GATT penalty or a rare Section 301 retaliation.

Higher penalties that might reduce the frequency with which this occurs are problematic because most executives benefit from the present system (another agency problem) and the ones that do not are worried that they will end up institutionalizing higher and more costly penalties that are no more effective.

In Chapter 5 we considered how the prospect of imperfect compliance information combines with the impact of uncertainty about state capacity to affect the design of a multilateral institution to reduce pollution in a common body of water. Two states, A and B, who are confident of each other's capability to implement the provisions of a regulatory agreement, must decide whether they want to invite a third less-developed state, C, to be part of their agreement. They are uncertain about the present capacity of the third state to insure that its industries comply with the agreement, and they are also concerned that the present capacity (whatever it might be) might deteriorate over time. The states are not comforted by the prospect that while they will be able to monitor the water's total pollution level, they will not be able to directly monitor each state's contribution to it.

States A and B are worried about state C's capacity to implement the terms of the treaty because they know that they might be better off in a bilateral agreement than in a trilateral one. This seems counterintuitive. Why should the implications of including state C in an agreement that it cannot stick to be worse than excluding it entirely? Is not the worst thing that can happen that state C acts as if the agreement never existed? Why not create a trilateral agreement and at least allow for the possibility that state C will be able to regulate its domestic industries? This may be a long shot, but it is unlikely to ever happen if state C is excluded from membership in the regulatory regime.

The fears of states A and B are, however, quite rational. They stem from a realization that a bilateral agreement with low enforcement costs can produce more benefits than a trilateral agreement with high enforcement costs. If state C does not have the capacity to institute the terms of the agreement, states A and B will have to punish it. In this case, this would necessitate both states relaxing the enforcement of their own domestic industries for some specified period of time— much in the way that the enforcement of a commodities cartel standard might lead a group of states to produce more in response to one state's suspected overproduction. Unfortunately, every time this is done both states would produce more pollution than if they were abiding by a bilateral agreement. If state C reneges on its agreement too often, the enforcement of the trilateral agreement will lead to more pollution than would exist if states A and B had formed a bilateral agreement instead and simply ignored state C's behavior entirely.

While the fears of states A and B might be justified in some circumstances, it remained to be seen how often this could be expected to be the case. The answer, it turns out, hinges on whether the states are simply uncertain about state C's present capacity or whether they are worried about its future capacity as well. Simulations suggest that the trilateral treaty could tolerate moderate amounts of uncertainty about state C's present capability. (Only when there is a significant probability that state C will violate the treaty immediately, will the bilateral treaty offer superior returns.) However, the expected benefits of the trilateral institution deteriorate dramatically when uncertainty about future capacity is added. Even modest levels of future capacity uncertainty interact with current uncertainty and imperfect observation to make it a losing proposition.

This theory suggests that the prevalence of uncertainty about the future capacity of developing and politically volatile states may provide part of the explanation for why such states are rarely members of international institutions with strongly enforced norms of cooperation but are frequently members of institutions where there is little or no enforcement of anything. It also suggests why oligopolistic institutions like commodity cartels and institutions whose task it is to regulate common pool resources are sometimes less aggressive in trying to insure universal participation than conventional collective goods theory would lead one to believe they should be. While free riders are costly, so is the punishment of states that do not have the capacity to comply with international norms—at least when the punishment requires that other members of the institution reduce their level of cooperation. Neither lesson should be lost on environmental activists who are trying to decide which states they should enlist to participate in a given regime.

Note that in each chapter the existence of domestic uncertainty in one form or another alters the character or operation of an institution to exert a significant effect on the international system. In the first case, limited access to information and constituency uncertainty about the extent to which the executive shares its preferences make it necessary for the constituency to evaluate the wisdom of a conflict decision solely on the outcome. This decision rule inspires executives to gamble for the resurrection of their political fortunes by prolonging or escalating losing conflicts beyond the point that would be supported by voters.

The net result is that domestic uncertainty leads to longer and more costly conflicts. Moreover, this effect does not vary. Unlike uncertainty about power or capability, which sometimes leads to a more peaceful world than would be obtained under perfect information and sometimes does not (Powell 1990), the effect of this domestic uncertainty *always* lies in the direction of provoking more conflict than would exist under full information.

Uncertainty about the timing and character of protectionist demands leads states to adopt enforcement sanctions that are far milder than those that would be necessary to enforce free trade. Nevertheless, this system works to the advantage of elected officials and protectionist interests, if not of the economy as a whole. The effect of this variety of domestic uncertainty is very difficult to excise from the international system. As we have just noted, if we move from a situation in which every state faces such protectionist interests to one in which most states are irrevocably committed to free trade but a significant number are not, the size of the sanction used to enforce the agreement cannot be increased proportionately. States with uncertainty about their protectionist demands have the greatest effect on the overall character of the regime. In a sense, domestic uncertainty tilts the entire regime toward its least cooperative common denominator.

Uncertainty about current and future state capacity affects the overall level of international cooperation by influencing the membership and distribution of international institutions. States with an uncertain capacity to enforce the norms of an institution or whose enforcement capacity is likely to change in an unknown way will tend to be excluded from institutions that enforce high levels cooperation. If they are admitted to a broad-based institution where cooperation is modest and voluntary, their incapacity will sabotage its subsequent evolution into something more ambitious. If too many states inspire assessments of high capacity uncertainty, there will be little deep cooperation at all. While uncertainty reduction is one of the greatest inspirations for institutions, high levels of capacity uncertainty can make their creation impossible.

6.2 Policy Prescriptions

The problems posed by these and other sources of domestic uncertainty do not easily yield to solution. Certainly, "democratization," the 1980s solution to everything that ails the international system—from too much conflict to too little economic growth—is by itself no answer.[1] Democratic states are, if anything, probably more prone than autocracies to gambling for resurrection behavior like moral hazard–generated escalation and diversionary war, and they are also prone to all sorts of instability generated by interest groups. This does not mean that one cannot discover many useful solutions to domestic uncertainty problems within democratic states. It only means that many of the solutions are likely to lie in the details of specific institutional structures and processes that vary across democracies and undoubtedly across autocracies as well. This complicates matters considerably, but as students of American and comparative politics know only too well, intelligent intervention in what we in international relations casually refer to as "domestic politics" is a messy and treacherous business. To begin the search for how domestic politics matters by comparing democracies and autocracies is sensible; to insist that this dichotomy—or a two-level ratification game—contains most of the answer is fatuous.

There are a variety of ways that polities might try to minimize the damage produced by constituency uncertainty about a chief executive's capabilities and motivations. One partial (and popular) remedy lies in the creation of institutional barriers such as the War Powers Act that prevent executives from unilaterally escalating the level of conflict or extending its duration. This strategy has much to recommend it, but experience has taught us that the information advantages that chief executives hold vis-à-vis their constituents do not necessarily disappear when they deal with legislators. Certainly, no legislature in the world has the same access to intelligence information as a chief executive does. To make matters worse, the ability of executives to circumvent formal requirements is extremely refined.

A more structural strategy is to minimize the amount of time that the executive has in which to gamble for resurrection. This can be done by installing a parliamentary system in which failures to win a vote of confidence can precipitate a new election. The adoption of a parliamentary system provides no guarantee that oversight and punishment will be conducted efficiently, however. Prime ministers, like presidents, can use their information advantage to understate the magnitude and significance of military setbacks and inflate the size and importance of victories. However, the ability of a parliamentary system to replace the

---

[1]Interesting critiques of these traditions can be found in Farber and Gowa (1994) and Przeworski and Limongi (1993).

executive relatively quickly gives it a clear advantage over a presidential system with fixed terms of office.

Still a third strategy involves the creation of institutions that support the emergence of an energetic and independent media. This acts to reduce the information advantages of executives both with regard to demonstrating the initial justifiability of conflict and with regard to estimating the success of military operations. An independent media also operates to "condition" voters to the possible incentives associated with diversionary war. If a population is cautioned about the likelihood of gambling for resurrection behavior in the face of a failing foreign intervention (or an economic recession), it will discount information used to justify the initiation of conflict and the value of the military successes that may follow. This will reduce the likelihood that such a strategy will be successful and, if an executive is aware of the diminished likelihood of success, it will also reduce the likelihood that gambling for resurrection will take place at all.

The prescriptive implications of knowing how domestic interest group uncertainty affects the design of free trade regimes are subtle. To appreciate them, one must first appreciate that a trade strategy based on the compensation standard or Tit-for-Tat cannot support free trade when there is uncertainty about interest group demands. By periodically responding to the domestic demands for protection and paying the compensation penalty, the government will find itself better off than if it had maintained free trade.

This does not mean, however, that leaders of a state interested in increasing free trade should respond to such a situation by fighting for large increases in the penalties for trade violations. The benefits that the executives of other states still obtain from periodically giving in to protectionist interests are likely to be too large to be offset by any politically feasible punishment.

When nontariff barriers are at issue, matters are even more complex. States cannot be certain whether apparent protection is state policy, incidental to a regulation in some other area, or a spillover from some traditional business or cultural practice. In the presence of such doubt, it is most efficient to employ a trigger strategy that considers the level of uncertainty before determining that a violation has been committed. This will have the effect of delaying the application of a sanction until there is a high degree of confidence that a violation has occurred and, like anything else that reduces the intensity or duration of the sanction, will result in a decrease in the total amount of cooperation that the treaty can generate.

Both sources of moderation are simple enough to understand intuitively, but they can present a big political problem for the chief executive and the official charged with insuring free trade. This is because moderation smacks of irresoluteness. Political opponents can always be expected to be absolutely certain that (1) harsher sanctions will bring greater rewards; and (2) any imbalance of trade is the product of a trade barrier. They will brush aside any rationalization based on either periodic increases in the intensity of interest group demands or the origins and magnitude of a barrier to trade. Unless the incumbent administration can explicate the benefits of avoiding costly but fruitless punishments and the trigger strategy rationale in a twenty-second sound bite or alternatively can somehow obscure the fact that such a strategy is being used (a prospect that is inconsistent with basic democratic principles) it may have to trade off economic efficiency for political survival.

The most important policy prescription of the chapter on state capacity is that we would do well to pay more attention to the problem of estimating the uncertainty connected with future state capacity changes. Uncertainty about future capacity acts to multiply the effect of the former in such away that it can easily operate to turn a moderately risky decision into a very poor one by dramatically increasing its potential cost.

Good policymakers know this intuitively. When they speak of capacity uncertainty in connection with Eastern Europe, Russia, or a developing state, they are invariably talking about the future as much as about the current situation. They also know better than most formal modelers that the prospect of uncertainty about state capacity will render short-term signaling strategies vis-à-vis costly commitments almost useless. There is no costly signal that Brazil can send that would instantly allay the fears of other states that macroeconomic mismanagement will return, nor is there a single signal that Russia could send that would convince Western Europe that it should be admitted to the European Union. Stability can only be demonstrated and uncertainty about capacity change can only be allayed over a significant period of time.

Because our analysis emphasizes the limitations of short-term signaling strategies for overcoming uncertainties about state capacity, it tends to corroborate the wisdom of offering states that are less administratively and political capable only qualified membership in regulatory institutions that demand a high degree of cooperation. Should they be admitted to full status, their inability to enforce the norms of the institution domestically would need to be sanctioned. This would increase the institution's costs and quite possibly lower its level of cooperative benefits, with the net result that the expanded institution might be less effective than its predecessor.

Even more damaging than the short-term consequences of such an expansion might be the damage it would do to the trajectory of an institution's cooperative evolution. Because the demands of more cooperative institutions are greater than those of less cooperative institutions and because harsher sanctions must be used to prevent states from defecting from their norms, the violations of less capable states increase in number and cost as an institution's level of cooperation increases. Hence, whenever a less capable state joins an institution, it reduces the likelihood that the institution will evolve toward greater cooperation.

The effect of uncertainty about capacity change does not mean, of course, that a strict regulatory institution with three member states will necessarily generate more cooperative benefits than will a weak institution with eighty members. Whether it will or not depends on the parameters of a given situation. What it does mean—and this is a message of each of the models in this book—is that the regime should be designed with the imperatives of domestic uncertainty in mind.

Bibliography

Abreu, Dilip. 1986. "Extremal Equilibria of Oligopolistic Supergames."
  Journal of Economic Theory 39: 191–225

Abreu, Dilip, David Pearce, and Ennio Stacchetti. 1986. "Optimal Cartel Equilibria with Imperfect Monitoring." *Journal of Economic
  Theory* 39: 251–269.

Alt, James E., Randall L. Calvert, and Brian D. Humes. 1988. "Reputation and Hegemonic Stability: A Game Theoretic Analysis."
  American Political Science Review 82: 445–67.

Alesina, Alberto, John Londregan, and Howard Rosenthal. 1993. "A
  Model of the Political Economy of the United States." *American
  Political Science Review* 87: 12–33.

Andressen, S. 1993. "The Effectiveness of the International Whaling
  Commission." *Arctic* 46: 108–15.

Aron, Raymond. 1973. *Peace and War*. Garden City, N.Y.: Anchor
  Books.

Axelrod, Robert. 1984. *The Evolution of Cooperation*. New York: Basic
  Books.

Babai, Don. 1993. "General Agreement on Tariffs and Trade." In Joel
  Krieger, ed. *The Oxford Companion to Politics*. New York:
  Oxford.

Banks, Jeffrey. 1991. *Signaling Games in Political Science*. New York:
  Harwood Academic Publishers.

Banks, Jeffrey, and Joel Sobel. 1987. "Equilibrium Selection in Signaling Games." *Econometrica* 55: 647–61.

Barzel, Yoram. 1977. "An Economic Analysis of Slavery." *Journal of
  Law and Economics* 20: 87–110.

———. 1982. "Measurement Cost and the Organization of Markets."
  Journal of Law and Economics 25: 27–48.

143

——. 1989. *Economic Analysis of Property Rights*. Cambridge: Cambridge University Press.

Bayard, Thomas O., and Kimberly Ann Elliott. 1994. *Reciprocity and Retaliation in U.S. Trade Policy*. Washington: Institute for International Economics.

Benoit, J. P., and V. Krishna. 1988. "Renegotiation in Infinitely Repeated Games." Cambridge, MA. Discussion paper.

Berkowitz, Bruce D. 1987. *Calculated Risks: A Century of Arms Control, Why It Has Failed, and How It Can Be Made to Work*. New York: Simon and Schuster.

Bernauer, Thomas. 1994. International Financing of Environmental Protection. Paper presented at the annual meeting of the American Political Science Association. Washington, D.C.

Bernheim, B. D., B. Peleg, and M. Whinston. 1987. "Coalition-proof Nash Equilibria." *Journal of Economic Theory* 42: 1–12.

Bernheim, B.D., and D. Ray. 1989. "Collective Dynamic Consistency in Repeated Games." *Games and Economic Behavior* 1: 295–326.

Betts, Richard K. 1987. *Nuclear Blackmail and Nuclear Balance*. Washington, D.C.: Brookings Institution.

Brams, Steven J. and D. Marc Kilgour. 1985. "Optimal Deterrence." *Social Philosophy and Policy* 3: 118–35.

——. 1988. *Game Theory and National Security*. New York: Basil Blackwell.

——. 1992. "Putting the Other Side 'On Notice' Can Induce Compliance in Arms Control." *Journal of Conflict Resolution* 3: 395–414.

Brodie, Bernard. 1965. *Strategy in the Missile Age*. Princeton: Princeton University Press.

Bueno de Mesquita, Bruce. 1985. "Toward a Scientific Understanding of Conflict." *International Studies Quarterly* 29: 121–36.

——. 1985. "The War Trap Revisited." *American Political Science Review* 79: 157–76.

Bueno de Mesquita, Bruce, and David Lalman. 1992. *War and Reason*. New Haven: Yale University Press.

Bueno de Mesquita, Bruce, Randolph Siverson, and G. Woller. 1992. "War and the Fate of Regimes: A Comparative Analysis." *American Political Science Review* 86: 638–46.

• Calvert, Randall. 1986. *Models of Imperfect Information in Politics*. New York: Harwood Academic Publishers.

⁰ ———. 1992. "Rational Actors, Equilibrium, and Social Institutions." Rochester, N.Y. Manuscript.

Carter, Ashton B. 1987. "Sources of Error and Uncertainty." In Ashton B. Carter et al., eds. *Managing Nuclear Operations.* Washington, D.C.: Brookings Institution.

Chayes, Abram, and Antonio Handler Chayes. 1990a. "Adjustment and Compliance Processes in International Regulatory Regimes," in Jessica T. Mathews, ed., *Preserving the Global Environment: The Challenge of Shared Leadership.* New York: Norton.

Chayes, Abram, and Antonio Handler Chayes. 1990b. "From Law Enforcement to Dispute Settlement." *International Security.* 14: 147–164.

Chayes, Abram, and Antonio Handler Chayes. 1993. *The New Sovereignty.* Cambridge, MA. Manuscript.

Cheung, Steven. 1974. "A Theory of Price Control." *Journal of Law and Economics* 12: 23–45.

⁰ ———. 1983. "The Contractual Nature of the Firm." *Journal of Law and Economics* 17: 53–71.

Clausewitz, Carl von. 1966. *On War.* London: Routledge.

Coase, Ronald H. 1937. "The Nature of the Firm." *Economica* 4: 386–405.

———. 1960. "The Problem of Social Cost." *Journal of Law and Economics* 3: 1–44.

———. 1988. *The Firm, the Market, and the Law.* Chicago: University of Chicago Press.

Commons, John. 1934. *Institutional Economics.* Madison: University of Wisconsin Press.

Cowhey, Peter F. 1993. "Domestic Institutions and the Credibility of International Commitment: Japan and the United States." *International Organization* 47(2): 299–326.

Deutsch, Karl, and J. David Singer. 1964. "Multipolar Power Systems and International Stability." *World Politics* 16: 390–406.

Devereux, Michael D., "Sustaining Free Trade in Repeated Games Without Government Commitment." British Columbia. Manuscript.

Dixit, Avinash. 1987. "Strategic Aspects of Trade Policy," in T. F. Bewley, ed., *Advances in Economic Theory: Fifth World Congress.* Cambridge: Cambridge University Press.

Downs, George, and David Rocke. 1990. *Tacit Bargaining, Arms Races, and Arms Control.* Ann Arbor: University of Michigan Press.

Downs, George, and David Rocke. 1994. "Conflict, Agency, and Gambling for Resurrection." *American Journal of Political Science* 38: 362–80.

Duffy, Gloria. 1988. "Conditions that Affect Arms Control Compliance." In Alexander George et al., eds. *U.S.-Soviet Security Cooperation.* New York: Oxford University Press.

Ellsberg, Daniel. 1972. *Papers on the War.* New York: Simon and Schuster.

Enthoven, Alain C., and Wayne K. Smith. 1971. *How Much Is Enough?* New York: Harper and Row.

Everitt, B. S., and D. J. Hand. 1981. *Finite Mixture Distributions.* New York: Chapman and Hall.

Farber, Henry, and Joanne Gowa. 1994. "Polities and Peace." Princeton. Manuscript.

Farley, John U., and Melvin J. Hinich. 1970a. "Detecting 'Small' Means Shifts in Time Series." *Management Science* 17: 189–99

Farley, John U., and Melvin J. Hinich. 1970b. "Testing for a Shifting Slope Coefficient in a Linear Model." *Journal of the American Statistical Association* 65: 1320–29.

Farley, John U., Melvin J. Hinich, and Timothy W. McGuire. 1975. "Some Comparisons of Tests for a Shift in the Slopes of a Multivariate Linear Time Series Model." *Journal of Econometrics* 3: 297–318.

Farley, Philip J. 1988. "Arms Control and U.S-Soviet Security Cooperation." In Alexander George et al., eds. *U.S.-Soviet Security Cooperation.* New York: Oxford University Press.

• Farrell, J., and E. Maskin. 1989. "Renegotiation in Repeated Games." *Games and Economic Behavior* 1: 327–60.

Fearon, James. 1994. "Domestic Political Audiences and the Escalation of International Disputes." *American Political Science Review* 88: 577–92.

Freedman, Lawrence. 1989. *The Evolution of Nuclear Strategy.* 2d ed. London: Macmillan.

√ Frieden, Jeffrey. 1991. "Invested Interests." *International Organization* 45: 425–451.

Friedman, J. 1971. "A Noncooperative Equilibrium for Supergames." *Review of Economic Studies* 38: 1–12.

Fudenberg, Drew, and Jean Tirole. 1991. *Game Theory.* Cambridge, Mass.: MIT Press.

Gaubatz, Kurt Taylor. 1991. "Election Cycles and War." *Journal of Conflict Resolution* 35: 212–44.

Gibbons, Robert. 1992. *Game Theory for Applied Economists*. Princeton: Princeton University Press.

Goldman, Emily. 1994. *Sunken Treaties*. University Park: Penn State Press.

Gray, Colin S. 1992. *House of Cards*. Ithaca, N.Y.: Cornell University Press.

Green, E., and R. Porter. 1984. "Noncooperative Collusion under Imperfect Price Information." *Econometrica* 52: 87–100.

Grossman, Gene, and E. Helpman. 1994. "Protection for Sale." *American Economic Review* 84: 833–50.

Grossman, Sanford, and Motty Perry. 1986. "Sequential Bargaining under Asymmetric Information." *Journal of Economic Theory*, 39: 120–54.

Hannan, E.J. and and Manfred Deistler. 1988. *The Statistical Theory of Linear Systems*. New York: John Wiley.

"Hard Road to Nuclear Waste Disposal, The." 1991. *Energy* 16: 19–21.

Harsanyi, John C. 1967–68. "Games with Incomplete Information Played by Bayesian Players." Parts 1–3. *Management Science* 14: 159–82, 320–34, 486–502.

Harsanyi, John C., and Reinhard Selten. 1988. *A General Theory of Equilibrium Selection in Games*. Cambridge, Mass.: MIT Press.

Harvey, A. C. 1981. *Times Series Models*. Oxford: Philip Allan.

Heider, F., 1958. *The Psychology of Interpersonal Relations*. New York: Wiley.

Helfat, Constance, and David Teece. 1987. "Vertical Integration and Risk Reduction." *Journal of Law, Economics, and Organization* 3: 47–68.

Hess, Gregory, and Athanasios Orphanides. 1994. "War Politics: An Economic, Rational Voter Framework." Manuscript.

Hibbs, Douglas. 1987. *The American Political Economy: Macroeconomics and Electoral Politics in the United States*. Cambridge, Mass.: Harvard University Press.

Hillman, Arye. 1989. *The Political Economy of Protection*. New York: Harwood Academic Publishers.

Hoffman, Stanley. 1968. *The State of War*. New York: Praeger.

Holsti, Oli R. 1972. *Crisis, Escalation, War*. Montreal: McGill-Queens University Press.

Huth, Paul. 1988. *Extended Deterrence and the Prevention of War.* New Haven: Yale University Press.

Iida, Keisuke. 1993. "When and How Do Domestic Constraints Matter?" *Journal of Conflict Resolution* 37: 403–26.

Jackman, Robert. 1994. *Power without Force.* Ann Arbor: University of Michigan Press.

Jackson, John. 1989. *The World Trading System.* Cambridge, Mass.: MIT Press.

———. 1990. *Restructuring the GATT System.* London: Royal Institute of International Affairs.

Jazwinski, Andrew H. 1970. *Stochastic Processes and Filtering Theory.* New York: Academic Press.

Jervis, Robert. 1976. *Perception and Misperception in International Politics.* Princeton: Princeton University Press.

———. 1978. "Cooperation under the Security Dilemma." *World Politics* 30: 167–214.

———. 1982–83. "Deterrence and Perception." *International Security* 7: 3–30.

get   ———. 1992. "Political Implications of Loss Aversion." *Political Psychology* 13: 187–204.

Kahneman, Daniel and Amos Tversky. 1979. "Prospect Theory: An Analysis of Decision under Risk." *Econometrica* 47: 263–91.

Kennan, George. F. 1951. *American Diplomacy, 1900–1950.* Chicago: University of Chicago Press.

Keohane, Robert O. 1984. *After Hegemony.* Princeton: Princeton University Press.

———. 1989. *International Institutions and State Power.* Boulder, Colo: Westview Press.

Keohane, Robert O., Peter Haas, and Marc A. Levy. 1993. "The Effectiveness of International Institutions." In Peter Haas, ed. *Institutions for the Earth* Cambridge, Mass.: MIT Press.

Kreps, David M. 1990. *A Course in Microeconomic Theory.* Princeton: Princeton University Press.

Kreps, David M., and Robert Wilson. 1982. "Reputation and Imperfect Information." *Journal of Economic Theory* 27: 253–79.

Lebow, Richard Ned, and Janice Gross Stein. 1989. "Rational Deterrence Theory: I Think Therefore I Deter." *World Politics* 41: 225–38.

Lehman, Howard P., and Jennifer L. McCoy. 1992. "The Dynamics of the Two-Level Bargaining Game." *World Politics* 44: 600–644.

Levinthal, Daniel. 1988. "A Survey of Agency Models of Organizations." *Journal of Economic Behavior and Organization* 9: 153–85.

Levite, Ariel, et al. 1992. *Protracted Military Interventions: From Commitment to Disengagement.* New York: Columbia University Press.

Levy, Jack S. 1992a. "An Introduction to Prospect Theory." *Political Psychology* 13: 171–86.

———. 1992b. "Prospect Theory and International Relations: Theoretical Applications and Analytical Problems." *Political Psychology* 13: 283–310.

Lippman, Walter. 1955. *Essays in the Public Philosophy.* Boston: Little-Brown.

Livermore, Seward. 1944. "Battleship Diplomacy in Latin America." *Journal of Modern History* 16: 31–48.

Machiavelli, Niccolo. 1950. *The Prince and the Discourses.* New York: Random House.

Maggi, Giovanni. 1994. "The Role of Multilateral Institutions in International Trade Cooperation," in *Essays on Trade Policy and International Institutions under Incomplete Information*, PhD Dissertation, Stanford University.

Marlin-Bennet, Renee, Alan Rosenblatt, and Jianxin Wang. 1992. "The Visible Hand." *International Interactions* 17: 191–207.

Martin, Lisa L. 1992. *Coercive Cooperation: Explaining Multilateral Economic Sanctions.* Princeton: Princeton University Press.

Maurer, John H. 1993. "The Anglo-German Naval Rivalry and Informal Arms Control, 1912–1914." *Journal of Conflict Resolution* 36: 284–308.

McCalla, Robert B. 1992. *Uncertain Perceptions.* Ann Arbor: University of Michigan Press.

Milgrom, Paul, Douglass North, and Barry Weingast. 1990. "The Role of Institutions in the Revival of Trade: The Medieval Law Merchant, Private Judges, and the Champagne Fairs." *Economics and Politics* 1: 1–23.

Milgrom, Paul, and John Roberts. 1990. "Bargaining Costs, Influence Costs, and the Organization of Economic Activity." In James Alt and Kenneth Schepsle, ed. *Perspectives on Positive Political Economy.* New York: Cambridge University Press.

———. 1993. *Economics, Organization, and Management.* New York: Prentice Hall.

Milner, Helen, and B. Peter Rosendorff. 1994. "Domestic Politics and International Cooperation: A Two-Level Signaling Game." New York. Manuscript.

Mitchell, Ronald. 1994. *Intentional Oil Pollution at Sea: Environmental Policy and Treaty Compliance.* Cambridge, Mass.: MIT Press.

Mo, Jongryn. 1994. "The Choice of Domestic Bargaining Regime in Two Level Games." Austin, Tex. Manuscript.

Morgenthau, Han J. 1973. *Politics among Nations.* New York: Knopf.

Morrow, James. 1991. "Electoral and Congressional Incentives and Arms Control." *Journal of Conflict Resolution* 35: 245–65.

———. 1993. "The Political Organization of International Trade." Stanford, CA, Manuscript.

———. 1994. *Game Theory for Political Scientists.* Princeton: Princeton University Press.

Myerson, Allen R. 1994. "New Limits Are Seen to Free Trade." *New York Times* (September 6).

Myerson, Roger B. 1991. *Game Theory.* Cambridge, Mass.: Harvard University Press.

Nalebuff, Barry. 1991. "Rational Deterrence in an Imperfect World." *World Politics* 43: 313–35.

Norpoth, Helmut, Michael Lewis-Beck, and Jean-Dominique Lafay. 1991. *Economics and Politics: The Calculus of Support.* Ann Arbor: University of Michigan Press.

North, Douglass. 1981. *Structure and Change in Economic History.* New York: Norton.

———. 1984. "Government and the Cost of Exchange." *Journal of Economic History* 44: 255–64.

———. 1990. *Institutions, Institutional Change and Economic Importance.* New York: Cambridge University Press.

North, Douglass, and Barry Weingast. 1989. "The Evolution of Institutions Governing Public Choice in 17th Century England." *Journal of Economic History* 49: 803–32.

Organski, A. F. K. 1968. *World Politics.* New York: Knopf.

Osborne, Martin J., and Ariel Rubinstein. 1994. *A Course in Game Theory.* Boston: MIT Press.

Oye, Kenneth A. 1992. *Economic Discrimination and Political Exchange.* Princeton: Princeton University Press.

Oye, Kenneth A., ed. forthcoming. *Specifying and Testing Theories of Deterrence.* Ann Arbor: University of Michigan Press.

Pearce, David. 1988. "Renegotiation-proof Equilibria." New Haven. Manuscript.

Persson, Torsten, and Guido Tabellini. 1990. *Macroeconomic Policy, Credibility, and Politics.* New York: Harwood Academic.

Pole, Andy, Mike West, and P. Jeff Harrison. 1988. "Nonnormal and Nonlinear Bayesian Modeling." in James C. Spall, ed. *Bayesian Analysis of Time Series and Dynamic Models.* New York: Marcel Dekker.

Porter, R. 1983. "Optimal Cartel Trigger-price Strategies." *Journal of Economic Theory* 29: 313–38.

Powell, Robert. 1990. *Nuclear Deterrence Theory.* New York: Cambridge University Press.

———. 1992. "Bargaining in the Shadow of Power." Berkeley, CA. Manuscript.

———. 1993. "Guns, Butter, and Anarchy." *American Political Science Review* 87: 115–32.

Przeworski, Adam, and Fernando Limongi. 1993. "Political Regimes and Economic Growth." *Journal of Economic Perspectives* 7: 51–69.

Putnam, Robert D. 1988. "Diplomacy and Domestic Politics: The Logic of Two-Level Games." *International Organization* 42: 427–60.

Rasmussen, Eric. 1989. *Games and Information.* Cambridge: Basil Blackwell.

Rodrik, Dani. 1989. "Promises, Promises: Credible Policy Reform via Signalling." *Economic Journal* 99: 756–72.

Roginko, Alexei. 1994. "Domestic Compliance with International Environmental Agreements." Manuscript.

Rogoff, Kenneth, and Anne Sibert. 1988. "Elections and Macroeconomic Policy Cycles." *Review of Economic Studies* 55: 1–16.

Ross, Lee, and Craig A. Anderson. 1982. "Shortcomings in the Attribution Process." In Daniel Kahneman, Paul Slovic and Amos Tversky, eds. *Judgment Under Uncertainty: Heuristics and Biases.* New York: Cambridge University Press.

Russett, Bruce. 1993. *Grasping the Democratic Peace.* Princeton: Princeton University Press.

Schear, James A. 1985. "Arms Control Compliance: Buildup or Breakdown?" *International Security* 10: 141–82.

Schelling, Thomas C. 1963. *The Strategy of Conflict.* New York: Galaxy Books.

————. 1966. *Arms and Influence*. New Haven: Yale University Press.

Schotter, Andrew. 1981. *The Economic Theory of Social Institutions*. Cambridge: Cambridge University Press.

Selten, Reinhard. 1978. "The Chain-Store Paradox." *Theory and Decision* 9: 127–59.

Smith, Alastair. 1994. "Foreign Policy and Reelection." Paper presented at the annual meeting of the Western Political Science Association. Albuquerque, New Mexico.

Snidal, Duncan and Andrew Kydd. 1993. "Progress in Game Theoretical Analysis of International Regimes." In Volker Rittberger, ed. *Regime Theory and International Relations*. New York: Oxford University Press.

Snider, Lewis. 1987. "Identifying the Elements of State Power: Where Do We Begin?" *Comparative Political Studies* 20: 314–56.

Staiger, Robert W. 1994. "International Rules and Institutions for Trade Policy." Madison, Wis. Manuscript.

Staw, Barry M. and Jerry Ross. 1991. "Understanding Behavior in Escalation Situations." *Science* 246: 216–20.

Stein, Arthur. 1982. "Coordination and Collaboration: Regimes in an Anarchic World." *International Organization* 36: 299–324.

Stein, Janice Gross. 1991. "Deterrence and Reassurance." In Philip Tetlock et al., eds. *Behavior, Society and Nuclear War*, Volume II. New York: Oxford University Press.

————. 1993. "International Cooperation and Loss Avoidance: Framing the Problems. In Janice G. Stein and Louis W. Pauly, eds. *Choosing to Cooperate: How States Avoid Loss*. Baltimore: Johns Hopkins University Press.

Stein, Janice, and Louis W. Pauly. 1993. *Choosing to Cooperate: How States Avoid Loss*. Baltimore: Johns Hopkins University Press.

Sun Tzu. 1991. *The Art of War*. London: Shambala.

Sykes, Alan O. 1990. "Mandatory Retaliation for Breach of Trade Agreements: Some Thoughts of the Strategic Design of Section 301." *Boston University International Law Journal* 8: 301–31.

————. 1991–92. "Constructive Unilateral Threats in International Commercial Relations: The Limited Case for Section 301." *Law and Policy in International Business* 23: 263–332.

Thucydides, 1954. *History of the Peloponnesian War*. New York: Penguin Books.

Tirole, Jean. 1990. *The Theory of Industrial Organization*. Cambridge, Mass.: MIT Press.

Titterington, D. M., A. F. M. Smith, and U. E. Makov. 1985. *Statistical Analysis of Finite Mixture Distributions*. New York: John Wiley.

Trachtenberg, Marc. 1991. *History and Strategy*. Princeton: Princeton University Press.

van Damme, Eric. 1989. "Renegotiation-proof Equilibria in Repeated Prisoner's Dilemma." *Journal of Economic Theory* 47: 206–7.

Waltz, Kenneth N. 1979. *Theory of International Politics*. New York: McGraw-Hill.

West, Mike, and P. Jeff Harrison. 1989. *Bayesian Forecasting and Dynamic Models*. New York: Springer.

Whittman, Donald. 1989. "Arms Control Verification and Other Games Involving Imperfect Detection." *American Political Science Review* 83: 923–45.

Williamson, Oliver E. 1975. *Market and Hierarchies: Analysis and Antitrust Implications*. New York: Free Press.

———. 1990. "Transaction Cost Economics." In Richard Schmalensee and Robert Willig, eds. *Handbook of Industrial Organization*. New York: North Holland.

Yarbrough, Beth V., and Robert M. Yarbrough. 1990. "International Institutions and the New Economics of Organization." *International Organization* 44: 235–259.

———. 1992. *Cooperation and Governance in International Trade*. Princeton: Princeton University Press.

Young, Oran R. 1989. *International Cooperation*. Ithaca: Cornell University Press.

Index

Abreu, Dilip, 80, 83
Adventurism, 60, 62, 64, 72
Alesina, Alberto, 57
Alt, James, 37, 39, 40
Anderson, Craig, 13
Andressen, S., 106
Aron, Raymond, 9, 12
Asset specificity, 20, 21
Asymmetric information, 24
Asymmetric preferences, 91–93
Attribution theory, 13
Autocracy, 139

Babai, Don, 87
Balance of Power, 11
Ball, George, 69, 70
Banks, Jeffrey, 27
Bargaining costs, 21
Barzel, Yoram, 21
Bayard, Thomas, 88, 135
Bayesian inferences, 28
Bayesian learning, 7
Bayesian updating, 31, 118, 119
Benoit, J.P., 83
Bernauser, Thomas, 106
Bernheim, D., 83
Bilateral agreement, 111, 112,
        125
Bipolarity, 11, 12

Brinkmanship, 10
Bueno de Mesquita, Bruce, 3,
        11, 12, 23, 66, 67

Calvert, Randall, 4, 27, 37, 39,
        40
Capability, 5, 6, 10–12
Capacity, 8, 9
Capacity change, 117–119
Capacity uncertainty, 107,
        114–120, 136, 137
    effects of, 121–123
Certainty effect, 15
Chain-store paradox, 35–37
Cheung, Steven, 21
Chicken (game), 10
Chief executive, 56–61, 63, 64,
        67–69, 71, 131–133,
        135–137, 139–141
Cholesky factor, 128
Coase, Ronald, 19, 21
Commons, John, 19
Compensation, 84, 91, 93, 96,
        100, 134
Compliance, 95, 105–107, 112,
        126, 136
Contraction, 124
Cooperation
    depth of, 107, 116

155

GEORGE W. DOWNS is the Professor of World Politics of Peace and War in the Department of Politics and the Woodrow Wilson School of Public and International Affairs at Princeton University. DAVID M. ROCKE is Professor in the Graduate School of Management and the Graduate Group in Statistics at the University of California, Davis. Downs and Rocke are the coauthors of *Tacit Bargaining, Arms Races, and Arms Control* (Michigan, 1990).